State Morality and a League of Nations

STATE MORALITY

AND

A LEAGUE OF NATIONS

STATE MORALITY

AND

A LEAGUE OF NATIONS

BY

JAMES WALKER

AND

M. D. PETRE

T. FISHER UNWIN, LTD.
LONDON : ADELPHI TERRACE

A729835

First Published in 1919

CONTENTS

FOREWORD

By M. D. PETRE

IN the following essays are set forth the views of
two friends, both of them democratic in senti-
ment, both of them ardently desiring such a
transformation of national and political life as
is implied in any scheme for a League of Nations,
but not agreed on the practical questions of its
fulfilment, and still less agreed in their view of
the essential characteristics of statecraft and
international policy. The first writer holds that
the end proposed may be achieved by purely
political action ; the second writer maintains that
political life has other aims and laws than those
of human idealism, and that its task in such
matters will be executive rather than initiative.
The one writer is imbued with the notion of the
state as a moral personality ; the other holds to
a more Machiavellian conception of the state

7

qua state—not to Machiavellism in the loose, popular meaning of the word, but to Machiavellism as the theory that politics have their own field of action, and that political morality is, indeed, a form of morality, but is not coextensive nor coprofound with human morality.

If these conflicting views were simply those of the two writers of this volume, their interest would not be far reaching ; but the reason for setting them forth in the way that has been done is that they probably present two undefined and opposite categories of thought on the subject before us, and on many kindred subjects of political interest.   Is the state to be regarded as a moral and Christian personality, according to the views of J.W. ?   Is it to be guided, in all things, by moral and human considerations ? Is it bound to the same purity and disinterestedness of conduct as a high-minded Christian ? Or has it, by reason of its very nature, a different and a less spiritual code of morality ?   Is a certain self-regard, that may run contrary to higher moral ideals, an essential element of its

constitution ?   Does its duty lie rather in leaving
room for the play of the nobler aspirations of
humanity than in actually forwarding them ?

Here are the two conflicting theories that
have been set forth in these pages, and their
interest is not merely academic, for if the first
theory be incorrect, then we shall waste much
time and incur much disappointment in trying
to obtain from state action what a state is not
calculated to produce. According to the
second theory, we shall trust in political action
only up to a certain point ; we shall not confide
in it for the full accomplishment of human
ideals ; we shall allow for state egotism so long
as states exist, and shall regard universal
brotherhood as a human rather than a political
ideal.   Politicians will only achieve what mankind in general will and desire.

Both views are in consonance with the idea of
a League of Nations, but they differ as to the
means of its accomplishment.

I

A LEAGUE OF NATIONS

I

A LEAGUE OF NATIONS

By JAMES WALKER

WITH the cessation of hostilities it becomes needful to form a more definite conception of what we mean by a League of Nations.

It is with causes as with men : we must beware when all seem to speak well of them. The absence of criticism must not be misinterpreted as an evidence that difficulties have been removed ; for the truth is that now that the champions of a League have been brought, by the resolute action of President Wilson, to the point of decision, difficulties are trooping out, not singly, but in battalions. In general it may be said that nearly everybody is agreed that a League which would secure, in time of international disputes, a reference of issues to an Arbitration Court or a Conciliation Council, and a pledge of common action against any Power

which failed to recognize this obligation, would
be a most desirable safeguard of peace and a
means of reducing the risk of war in the future.
But it would be idle to minimize the fact that,
even amongst those who cherish this ideal, there
are many who doubt whether it can be translated into practice.   There are those who fear
that the warlike instincts of races cannot be
subjugated.   Man, it is said, is by nature a
fighting animal, in proof of which it is pointed
out that every previous attempt to secure the
world's peace has failed, and in the end nations
have fallen back helplessly upon the theory that
so long as human nature is human nature there
will be from time to time wars and rumours of
wars.   War, it is said, is a fatality from which
there is no escape.

" Some day the live coal behind the thought,
    Whether from Baal's stone obscene
    Or from the shrine serene
Of God's pure altar brought,
Bursts up in flame ; the war of tongue and pen
    Learns with what deadly purpose it was fraught,
    And helpless in the fiery passion caught,
Shakes all the pillared state with shock of men."

What chance is there that the sentiments which are being freely expressed to-day in favour of a League will succeed any better than those that were widely held in Europe at the close of the Napoleonic War? There is hardly an emotion roused by present horrors that did not find expression by our forefathers a hundred years ago in much the same terms. If, for instance, we compare the utterances of President Wilson with those of the Duc de Sully at the beginning of the seventeenth century, or with those of the Abbé de St. Pierre after the Congress of Utrecht in 1713, or with the views of Kant in "Eternal Peace," or, more particularly, with the speeches of the "Crowned Jacobin" Tsar Alexander I., the creator of the Holy Alliance, we shall find that all our new thoughts have thrilled dead bosoms, that the hopes we cherish to-day have proved vain in the past. Like President Wilson, Tsar Alexander believed, with strong conviction, that the only possible basis for a permanent system of peace was the reorganization of Europe on strictly

national lines. "Why," he asked, "could
one not submit to it [a congress] the positive
rights of nations, assure the privilege of neutrality, insert the obligation of never beginning
war until all the resources which the mediation
of a third party could offer have been exhausted,
until the grievances have by this means been
brought to light, and an effort to remove them
has been made? On principles such as these
one could proceed to a general pacification and
give birth to a League, of which the stipulations
would form, so to speak, a new code of the law
of nations, which, sanctioned by the greater
part of the nations of Europe, would without
difficulty become the immutable rule of Cabinets,
while those who should try to infringe it would
risk bringing upon themselves the forces of the
new union."

This was said in 1804, and it is precisely what
our leaders repeat to-day. But it was not a
mere expression of opinion, it was translated
into action. In 1814, when Europe was sick
unto death of war, the Tsar's plan was adopted

by the Congress of Vienna, and later on the famous Holy Alliance, the first League of Nations, formed to secure peace, came into being. Men's hopes ran high in those days. "They promised themselves," said a delegate to the Congress, "an all-embracing reform of the political system of Europe, securities for peace—in short, the return of the Golden Age." There is not a single belligerent in the present war that does not cherish the same hope. Lord Robert Cecil declares that a League of Nations is the only thing worth fighting for; Mr. Balfour says it is his ideal aim; and Captain Persius and Count Czernin have endorsed the statement that it is only by such a League, accompanied with a measure of disarmament, that Europe can be saved from ruin. Even the German Government has been compelled to accept the principle, and some of its leaders have actually gone farther than British statesmen by recommending that the League shall use its force, not only against any Power that refuses to submit a dispute to the Tribunal,

2

but also against any Power that refuses to accept
a decision. Are these hopes doomed to share
the fate of the Holy Alliance? Will a League
of Peace again prove impracticable? Will
those who bless it to-day be compelled to admit
ten or twenty years hence that, like the Holy
Alliance, it was "a piece of sublime mysticism
and nonsense".?

Before attempting to deal with these questions I must outline another series of doubts
that are likely to be urged when the League of
Peace comes up for detailed discussion. It will
be said by critics that, human nature being what
it is, strong nations will never submit to be
cribbed, cabined, and confined within the
corners of another scrap of paper. Like
Germany they will plead that the insurgent spirit
of their will-to-power, being a vital manifestation, a legitimate and natural impulse of growth,
is primarily a higher law of conduct than a
pledge given under different circumstances ten,
twenty, or even fifty years ago. "The letter
killeth, but the spirit giveth life." Why, it is

asked, should one generation be bound by contracts entered into by their forefathers, after those contracts have ceased to serve the laws of growth and have become a handicap to free development and expansion? What may be prudent and serviceable to-day may be obsolete ten years hence. A scheme of treaties and pledges that would perpetuate a *status quo* and admit of no change would be simply a death-trap. Strong nations would destroy it rather than succumb to it. This is Germany's argument to-day, but every nation has pleaded it at one time or another. It is, in fact, the chief contention of Professor Wilkinson in his work "Government and the War," where he argues that no process of law or of arbitration can deal with the phenomenon of growth, because any tribunal administering a system of right or law must base its decision upon the tradition of the past, which has become unsuited to the new conditions that have arisen. The growing state is necessarily expansive or aggressive. For this reason he argues that "peace cannot rationally be the object of policy.'' A state must seek to promote its own efficiency, growth, and expansion, and, when challenged, it must choose between war and the sacrifice of what makes life worth living. Is not this British Bernhardi-ism ? Could not Germany plead it, as in fact she did, as an excuse for the violation of Belgium's neutrality ? And how can those who hold such views condemn Bethmann Hollweg for dismissing, as a scrap of paper, a Treaty which was considered inimical to the growth of Germany ? Surely on their theory Germany was right in seeking war, and they come perilously near hypocrisy in condemning her in one breath while inculcating her principles in the next.

Against all this the advocates of a League of Nations must challenge as false any interpretation of human nature which assumes that it is irremediably bad and wholly selfish ; that pessimism is a fact while optimism is merely a dream ; that the life of nations is to be measured in terms of the lowest denominator. Man is a great deal more than a fighting animal, and in that more lie all his hopes and good. He must be considered not merely in relation to his antecedent failures, but even more closely in relation to his actual achievements, and, above all, in relation to his aim. He has a power of self-determination by the exercise of which he is able to change his nature radically. He outgrows habits, customs, tastes; he can and does develop latent and unsuspected potentialities. If we are ever to have a League of Nations worthy the name we must get rid of the notion that human nature is necessarily against it. In every sphere of human activity examples will be found of the simple truth that progress is made in defiance of past experience, by the faith and resolution of men and nations who refuse to accept the defeat and frustration of their hopes.

"*Then,*" said Christian, "*I must venture. To go back is nothing but death; to go forward is fear of death and life everlasting beyond it. I will yet go forward.*"

To how many men in the trenches, hemmed
in under deadly attack, has this dilemma presented itself ?   But it is not only the occasion
for heroism on the battlefield, but the whole
duty of those of us at home.   We, too, must
venture as they have ventured, for they without
us may not be made perfect.   They have
fought for ideals which we must translate into
realities, and if we fail to make a great effort to
establish a League of Nations, such as will give
a safeguard against a renewal of present
horrors, we betray them.   The world would in
that event backslide into the vicious circle of
increasing armaments, antagonistic alliances,
secret diplomacy—and this is the way of death.
This dire alternative should be the supreme
incentive impelling the nations to seek a new
way of life, and energizing them with the moral
courage to overcome the inertia of mind and
imagination which has led them in the past to
worship ''the God of things as they are.''   If
those who say that a League of Nations is
impracticable merely because it is difficult will

consider that the only alternative is not peace, but an armed truce culminating in another Armageddon, they will surely pluck up faith to make the effort necessary to avert such a catastrophe.

And this war, rightly regarded, should give them grounds for hope and confidence. For, say what they may, it has not occurred because man is a fighting animal. It is not primarily an ebullition of innate depravity. Nor has it been caused by an attempt to interfere with the laws of growth. It has occurred because a great nation deliberately *willed* it. The disclosures of Lichnowsky and Muehlon are conclusive on this point. Germany has not fought in response to an irresistible instinct, or because she naturally and spontaneously loves fighting. Nor has she fought, as her apologists pretend, under the impulse of biological necessity. She went to war *because she made herself wish to do so*, because every phase and department of her national life, over a long period, was designed by human effort to conform to this will to war.

And the question arises—Is it not possible for
the world to will peace more strongly than it
was possible for one nation to will war, and also
to bring to the support of the effort a mightier
array of power and device ?   Surely the greater
probability is that nations can do this if only
they make up their minds to try.

But there must be a new orientation of
thought and effort.   Before the war approxim-
ately 700 books dealing with war as a science
and "a biological necessity" were published in
Germany every year, whereas throughout the
world there was not more than a small fraction
of this number of books dealing with peace.
" If one hundredth part of the consideration and
thought that has been given to this war is given
to schemes of peace," says General Smuts,
"then you will never see war again."   It was
because the stronger national bias in Europe
was set towards war that war came.   If the
greater bias had been towards peace, if the plans
to secure and maintain it had been as well
thought out as the intrigues to break it, if the

champions of a League of Nations had been as clever and resolute and sincere as the German militarists, there would have been no war. And this bias, it should be remembered, is controllable and determinable by human effort. The war was not a fatality. It has arisen in the will of man, and when that will has been definitely focussed and concentrated in the opposite direction we shall secure a peace worth having. In the past the Great Powers have never really chosen peace unreservedly. Some have tried to do so with more sincerity than others, but eventually they have been thwarted by the action of·Powers who acted in a contrary sense. There is to-day such an opportunity as the world has never had of making a fresh start with a definite choice of peace and a general pledge to work and fulfil it. *Pace* Professor Wilkinson, we must begin by making peace the object of national policy. We must entrench around it and fortify the position with as much skill and energy as we have in the past prepared for war. We should adopt the bold suggestion of the late Lord Parker by entering into an understanding that each member of the League should agree, in its elementary schools and other schools, to inculcate, as far as may be, the desirability of settling international disputes on principles of right and justice and not by force of arms.   We must bring our whole life into focus with this aim, and organize measures to secure peace as thoroughly as we have organized the methods of waging and winning a war.   This is real self-determination which means, not the liberty to do what we like, but the power to make a deliberate choice and then conform our national activities to it.

We must, however, discard the fallacy that the only way to secure peace is to prepare for war.   For this is tantamount to an admission that evil is the only positive force and can only be averted by evil.   It means, in effect, that instead of really strengthening the desire for peace we increase the fear of evil, until it becomes an irresistible obsession to which one or another of the nations succumbs.   All experience warns us that we can only overcome evil finally by good ; our love of peace must be so strong that war ceases to attract. This is not only true religion, but also sound psychology. The greatest evils that mankind has grappled with were not all defeated in open combat, but most frequently by the development of contrary desires, which finally resulted in a diversion of human energy, thereby robbing the evils of their attraction and power to do mischief. And beyond doubt if war ever becomes a thing of the past it will be by virtue of the triumph of a similar process. The efforts that have been made to regulate the hateful thing must be diverted to the more important task of creating conditions under which it will become increasingly difficult and ultimately almost impossible for it to recur.

In the meantime, however, the promoters of a League of Nations must address themselves to the most immediate phases of the problem. For the present the League could not, in the

nature of things, guarantee, even if the most
sanguine hopes were fulfilled, that there would
be no more wars, nor could it dispense with the
weapons of material force.   President Wilson
is very explicit on this point.   He has avowed
his conviction that it is absolutely necessary to
create as guarantor of the authority of the
League a force "so much greater than the force
of any nation now engaged, or any alliance
hitherto formed or projected, that no nation, no
probable combination of nations, could face or
withstand it.   If the peace presently to be made
is to endure, it must be made secure by the
organized major force of mankind."   Clearly,
there is no assumption here that all nations will
become pacifists after this struggle.   The
great hope is that ultimately enlightened self-
interest can be harmonized with the dictates of
right and reason ; that just as it is more prudent
for the individual to observe the law rather than
incur the penalties of lawless self-seeking, so in
the case of a nation it will be better in the long
run to conform to the laws of nations than to

break them. It is confidently anticipated that one of the results of the war will be the conscious coming of self-interest throughout the world to the support of morality in the relations of nations as of men. When nations find that war does not pay, they will be less prone to resort to it. When they realize that the only way in which they can gain security is to guarantee the security of their neighbours, there should be created an atmosphere in which the League of Nations would become entirely practicable. "As footpads, safe-breakers, burglars, and incendiaries are suppressed in nations," said Viscount Grey, "so those who would commit these crimes, and incalculably more than these crimes, will be suppressed." But for many decades covenants without the sword will be but words; behind the law there must be power to enforce it. This was the lesson of the Hague Tribunal, which failed to save Europe in 1914 because it had no power to enforce its agreements. This risk will not be incurred again.

Those who expect that a League of Peace will involve total disarmament are therefore imagining a vain thing. It should, of course, result in an immense reduction of armaments, and when it is thoroughly established it would assert itself to ensure that no nation should possess armaments that appear to be in excess of its actual requirements, and that all private capitalistic influences in the expansion of armaments should be eliminated. All the belligerents are committed under President Wilson's Points to the principle of limitation of armaments, and he has further explained that what he means by this principle is that armies and navies will be, in future, "a power for order merely, not an instrument of aggression or of selfish violence." Herr Erzberger, in the draft scheme outlined in the Press, which is understood to embody the views of the new German Government on the subject, insists that the Powers of the League "must undertake not to use their forces for any other objects than the maintenance of international order, for defence against attack on their territory, and for the joint executive work of the League." And, further, he suggests that an account of armaments expenditure, with complete particulars, shall be furnished annually to the League's Bureau at the Hague for general publication. This, of course, would be a very delicate matter. But the agreement between Britain and Germany regarding a fixed ratio of capital ships before the war is a precedent that should be capable of extended application in the future ; and, furthermore, the League would be in a strong position to satisfy any Power, in fear of aggression, of the most formidable safeguards. Until men found that the law gave them adequate security they went about armed, and nations will do the same ; but in the end the League of Nations would, in the measure of its success, tend to supersede the necessity for such precautions, until finally they would disappear.

When we turn to inquire what is President Wilson's special contribution to the League of Nations propaganda we find that, beyond

impassioned appeals for acceptance of the
principle, and frequent avowals that it is the
supreme aim of America's policy, he has not
propounded a definite scheme.   He has enunci-
ated principles, but has not yet translated them
into concrete proposals.   As a matter of fact
Lord Bryce, the Fabian Society, the Labour
Party, and other persons and groups on this
side of the Atlantic have been much more
explicit.   President Wilson, however, appears
to have accepted the proposals of the American
League to enforce peace, which, up to a point,
are practically on all fours with other schemes
familiar to the public.   This League proposes
that justiciable issues—that is to say, disputes
regarding international law and the interpretation of treaties arising between members of
the League—shall be referred to an International Court for decision, and that non-justiciable issues affecting the honour and vital
interests of a nation, which have generally been
excluded from arbitration treaties and do not
admit of settlement by legal methods, shall be

referred to a Council of Conciliation for investigation and report. It is also provided that Signatory Powers shall jointly use forthwith their military and economic forces against any one of their number that goes to war, or commits acts of hostility against another of the Signatories, before the issue in dispute has been submitted to one or other of the foregoing tribunals.

Both America and Britain have already furnished proof of their sincere adherence to these principles in Treaties entered into before the war. In 1908, for instance, they agreed to refer justiciable cases between them to the Hague Tribunal, and in 1914 they went farther and entered into a Treaty to submit even non-justiciable cases affecting their honour and vital interests to a permanent International Commission, pledging themselves not to go to war during such an investigation and before the Commission had submitted its report. These Treaties constitute a nucleus for a larger scheme into which all the present Allies may be drawn after the war. If the two greatest Powers in the world can safely enter into such far-reaching compacts, there can hardly be any insuperable difficulties against smaller Powers, with a narrower range of interests, following their example ; and if members of the League are agreed to concede each other certain economic privileges, other Powers might sooner or later be compelled to apply for admission, accepting its terms and limitations in return for its safeguards. Indeed, if the whole of the present Allies were to form themselves after the war into a League to enforce peace, it would be almost impossible for the rest of the world to stand aloof, for Britain and America and their Allies could control the raw materials of three-quarters of the world. This would be the mightiest weapon in the armoury of the League, and if it were honestly used for one supreme purpose—namely, the suppression of aggression and the enforcement of peace in the interests of humanity—it could never become a tyranny.

Reverting to the general principle of the

American League, several obvious criticisms suggest themselves. The League, it appears, does not commit the Signatories to the use of force against a Power that refuses to accept its decision. Its pains and penalties are reserved, not for those who go to war, but only for those who go to war without first submitting their case to the Court or the Conciliation Council. Punishment is for refusal to discuss and submit for judgment, not for aggression. Thus, if we suppose such a League to have been in actual operation in 1914, the Central Powers could have frustrated it by agreeing that their case against Serbia should be referred for consideration. They would have disarmed the League, so to speak, by going so far, and then, no matter what the decision, they would be free to go to war without let or hindrance. This is simply arbitration without any obligation to abide by the decision. It must be assumed, however, that the League would not acquiesce in practice to such a humiliation. Because the Signatories are not pledged to compel acceptance of their

decision in formal terms the omission is not
perhaps an oversight, but rather a provision
which leaves the final decision regarding war to
each national government instead of to a super-
state authority.   Nevertheless, it seems necessary, if the scheme is to be well and truly laid,
that a proviso should be included for further
action in the case of a Signatory who, after
receiving the decision of the Tribunal, refuses
to abide by it ; otherwise the League could not
strictly fulfil President Wilson's avowed aim
"to guarantee peace and justice throughout
the world."   Justice cannot be done merely by
pronouncing a decision and leaving it optional
to the parties to reject it without penalties.   Nor
could peace be wholly guaranteed if, under the
terms of the League, Powers were free, of
course at their own risk, to refuse to accept a
judgment of the League.   There is, in truth,
only one way in which all that the President
hopes could be attained, and that is by treating
as an act of war against the League not only
refusal to wait for judgment, but also resistance

to a judgment.   Without the latter there could
be no absolute guarantee of justice, but only a
guarantee that there shall be no war between
Signatories without full submission and examination of the issue.

A further omission, for which no explanation
can be offered, is that the American scheme does
not compel Signatories to bring their disputes to
the Court or the Tribunal ; it simply says that
they must not go to war before submitting them.
This, of course, offers a wide field for intriguing
aggression.   Disputes may be allowed to drag
on for years while secret preparations for war
are in progress, and then the aggressor, at his
own selected moment, may refer the matter to
the League merely in order to disarm it after
decision has been delivered and rejected.   The
League must not only have power to compel
delay and full discussion, it must, if it is to
be effective, have power to hale an offender into
Court, require a Power to bring forward a
specific issue that may threaten trouble, and
also to summon a suspect Power to explain its

conduct. In other words, the League must not only have adequate powers to overcome a crisis, but full authority to intervene in good time to prevent one. Intervention is rarely serviceable when made at the last moment of the eleventh hour. Time must be taken by the forelock in such matters.

Germany, for instance, might very properly have been required by a League to explain her action in 1913 in suddenly making a levy of capital for £50,000,000 for special military requirements. This was an unprecedented extra Budget demand for which no satisfactory explanation was given at the time, and, of course, it compelled France and Russia to follow suit with supplementary army laws. Again, Germany might have been asked by a League to give reasons for the fear of "encirclement" which played such a prominent part, long before 1914, in her war propaganda.

The American scheme, as originally outlined, contains no such proposal, but the projected Treaty drafted by Lord Bryce and others con-

tains clauses which provide safeguards on this
point.   Where, in the opinion of the Conciliation
Council, any dispute exists between Signatory
Powers, or where it appears to the Council that
the good relations between them are likely to be
endangered, the Council may make suggestions
and invite each Power to state its case.   This
clause is of great importance because, if
adopted and wisely applied, it would afford a
means for the revision of Treaties and a readjustment of the *status quo* on evidence being produced that such a change would tend to safeguard the world's peace.   Means must be
devised whereby Treaties may from time to time
be reviewed and revised to meet the exigencies
of changed circumstances.

A further, and scarcely less important, advantage inherent in this clause is that it could be
applied so as to frustrate the methods of secret
diplomacy.   The Conciliation Council could
educate the world by giving out reliable and
impartial information regarding problems and
dangers that the Powers concerned might wish

to keep vague and undefined. It would publish suggestions which could not be lightly dismissed as ex-parte statements. It might, in fact, prove in practice a great instrument for the creation of a sound and enlightened public opinion regarding foreign affairs. In every speech on the subject President Wilson has recognized that the League must have done with the traditional method of secret diplomacy, and he cannot, therefore, have overlooked the extent to which the Conciliation Council could contribute to this result. "This partnership" (the League of Nations), he has said, "must be a partnership of peoples, not a mere partnership of Governments"; and this can only mean that the terms upon which the new order is to be founded must be fully and frankly discussed and approved by the Parliaments of the Signatory Powers.

One of the strongest arguments against a League to enforce peace is that it must necessarily restrict the sovereign rights of Signatory Governments and threaten the whole theory of national independence. There cannot be an

effective super-state authority without a con-
comitant limitation of the independence of states.
A partner can never have quite the same liberty
as a sole proprietor ; he must act up to the
terms of the partnership deed.   States that form
the League, it is said, will be no longer masters
in their own house.   They may be assured at
the outset that there will be no vexatious intervention in their internal affairs, but in practice
it will be found impossible to make a distinction
between external affairs that are a legitimate
concern of a League, and "internal affairs
having an external effect."   Perhaps the most
effective reply is that this danger can hardly be
so serious or the United States would not be
favourable to a League.   No nation is so
passionately devoted to the principle of independence as the Americans. It is their dominant
political inspiration, and they are the last people
in the world to submit to the vexatious interference of other Powers.   But America and
probably every other Power in the world has
been taught by the lessons of this war that the

atomistic conception of inter-state society, the
notion that a state can remain isolated and
neutral when a challenge is thrown down to every
principle of civilization, is simply untenable.
"We are participants," says President Wilson,
"whether we would or not, in the life of the
world.   The interests of all nations are our own
also.   We are partners with the rest.   What
affects mankind is inevitably our affair as well as
the affair of the nations of Europe and of Asia."
Every state has international as well as national
interests.   Humanity is greater than any nation,
and a Power that ignores its claims and remains
aloof and neutral when they are jeopardized will
soon find that its national interests have suffered
a marked depreciation.

America, at any rate, has found that aloof-
ness from European affairs is no longer possible,
and, as a corollary, she could not deny the rights
of Europe to intervene in a similar crisis within
her borders.   This means that the old conception of the Monroe Doctrine has been thrown
into the melting-pot.   America has departed

from her traditional policy. She has inter-
vened, and thereby admits the right of intervention, and this is her greatest contribution to the
League of Nations. For the sake of humanity
and internationalism she has made a sacrifice of
her traditions. But although the Monroe Doctrine, as conceived by generations of Americans,
appears to have been discarded, it may yet
emerge in a new form in a wider field. In a
recent address to the Senate President Wilson
explained : '' I am proposing, as it were, that
the nations should with one accord adopt the
doctrine of President Monroe as the doctrine of
the world—that no nation should seek to extend
its policy over any other nation or people, but
that every nation should be left free to determine
its policy, its own way of development, unhin-
dered, unthreatened, unafraid, the little along
with the great and powerful.'' But, presumably, although President Wilson would not be
willing to allow any single Power to interfere
with another's '' own way of development,'' he
would not deny that the League should have the

right of intervention where a country is reduced to such a state of chaos by bad government that it becomes a menace to its neighbours. He must have had the case of Mexico in his mind, and although his attitude in this matter should be clearly defined, it may be assumed, from the implications involved in his decisions, that the right of intervention by the League would be asserted in all internal disputes that threaten to have a disruptive effect upon the general relations of the League. Where, as in the case of the Irish problem, the trouble is strictly localized, the national Government concerned may be left to settle it ; but where a dispute cannot be localized, and threatens to extend to other nations, the League must assert a right to be consulted through its Conciliation Council.

Here I must pause to consider an important series of objections which Mr. Belloc has formulated against some of the current schemes. His main contention is that patriotism, or the idea of nationality, is so strong that no great

Power will acquiesce in the derogation from sovereignty involved in the entrance into a League. "No man," he says, "will die for the abstraction of an International State. But an Englishman will die for England, a Jew will die for Israel, a Frenchman will die for France. That is the root fact that you cannot get over." This argument brings us back to the old contention that the League proposals are against human nature. It must be pointed out, however, that the force of Mr. Belloc's contention is derived from the assumption that it is the immediate aim of the promoters of the League to create an International State, whereas the fact is that none of the most important schemes go so far. The time may come when such a State may be formed, but at present it is too remote to be considered within the sphere of practical politics. Mankind is not ripe for such a vast experiment, and, therefore, we must be content with something less ambitious and less difficult of achievement. A League of Nations may ultimately become the nucleus for an International State, but as at present conceived it is a much more modest proposal. Such international tribunals as are necessary will be the creation of the Powers who agree to recognize them, and, far from covering the whole range of any State's affairs, they will be concerned with one specific object, the maintenance of peace. The only sovereign right that a Power entering the League will be required to abandon is the right, if it be right at all, to make war as it pleases, to impose its will upon others by armed force. It is utterly unconvincing to contend that if a state forfeits this dubious right it must sign away its birthright, lose its sovereignty, and sink to the level of an obscure province, for it will still remain in supreme authority over a thousand interests much more vital to its independence. Will anyone be so bold as to argue that because individuals have, for the most part, abandoned the methods of violence in their dealings with one another, and have ceased to steal what they want, and murder those who stand in their way, they have thereby forfeited their independence

for an absurd abstraction? The suggestion
will not survive a moment's analysis. Great
laws are not fetters, but the conditions of real
freedom. "Restraints laid by a people on
itself," says Landor, "are sacrifices made to
liberty; and it never exerts a more beneficent
or a greater power than in imposing them." It
may be true, as Mr. Belloc writes, that no man
will die for the abstraction of an International
State, but men will die, and have died in this
war by tens of thousands, for the cause of
humanity, for justice and righteousness. It is
indeed an insult to the Allies to pretend that
patriotism in its narrowest sense—"My country
right or wrong"—has been the dominant
inspiration of the Allied armies, and that there
is no difference between their motives and
those that have animated Prussian militarism.
Patriotism is not enough; Englishmen will die
for other things besides England. Limitation
of sovereignty is not peculiar to a League of
Nations; it arises in all international relations,
but chiefly in the affairs of democracies, where

the necessity for self-limitation in the interests
of humanity is, or should be, most generally
admitted. Neither in Britain nor in America
was it successfully urged that the arbitration
Treaties which, as suggested, may form the
nucleus of a League, would involve a loss of vital
independence. Nor was this plea urged with
any conviction against the submission during the
last century of no fewer than 471 international
disputes to arbitration, simply because civilized
Powers have ceased to regard as derogatory
to their independence a self-imposed limitation
made in the general interests of humanity. They
have come to recognize tacitly, if not overtly,
that this is the higher way of life prepared for
us by Him "whose service is perfect freedom,"
and that it leads, if we will but follow fearlessly,
to the dawn of an ampler day.

It is not then, primarily, to an International
State that nations are asked to submit, but to
the principle *securus judicat orbis terrarum* in
international affairs. They are not required to
sign away their birthright, but to admit the

absolute supremacy of the moral law in their relations. In a word, they are asked to surrender the claim to regard themselves as absolute autocrats in favour of what President Wilson has aptly termed "the organized opinion of mankind." And a patriotism which will not make this concession, which prates against the horrors of militarism, but will not lift a finger to remove them, which exalts sovereignty into a fetish more exacting than any international abstraction and more autocratic than any personal autocrat—what, indeed, is this thing but "the last refuge of scoundrels"? It is nothing less than the foul idol of Prussian militarism disguised in a top hat and a frock coat.

Closely allied to Mr. Belloc's objections is another group, of which we shall hear a good deal as the controversy proceeds. There are Junkers in all the Allied countries who hold the extreme Prussian view that war is "God's own medicine." The theory is disguised in various forms. Sometimes war is presented as a glorious venture in which all heroic qualities find

scope on the grandest scale ; at other times it is
offered as a mighty purge from all that is
feeble and decadent ; or, again, it is urged
that, say what we may, war restores ethical
elements without which civilization would
decay. "Eternal peace," said Moltke, "is a
dream, and not even a beautiful dream." It
is a sort of *nirvana* in which nations lapse into
impotence, somnolence, and cowardice. One
of Mr. Wells's characters puts the matter
thus : "War is an activity. Peace is not. If
you take war out of world you must have some
other activity. . . . A World-State or a
League of Nations with nothing to do but to keep
the peace will bore men intolerably." Now all
these plausible sophistries spring from a confusion of the terms "war" and "conflict," from
regarding the two things as absolutely synony-
mous, and from failure to recognize their important differences. Conflict is unquestionably a
law of life, and without it men and nations tend
to drift into a state of stagnation. But the
elimination of war does not involve a cessation

of conflict. If war were abolished to-morrow there would remain a host of conflicts, for nations as for individuals. Man has to struggle for a livelihood, for moral and spiritual development against all the forces of darkness and ignorance. There is conflict everywhere between opposing principles and powers throughout nature. "All life," said Charles Booth, "rests upon a balance of forces. We stand or walk or fall, morally and economically as well as physically, by management or mismanagement of conflicting forces." Even the sanity of a State has been defined as the balance of a thousand insanities. But war is only one form of conflict, not the whole. It is a species, not a genus. And the special character which distinguishes it from forms of legitimate conflict is that it is, as Clausewitz said, "an act of violence," or, as defined by Grotius, "*certatio per vim.*" Such violence, however, is only an incident in a permanent process of conflict between powers, beliefs, and personalities in the world. When men surrendered the prac-

tice of settling their differences by personal combat, with swords and pistols, they did not finally
eliminate the principle of conflict from their
affairs ; nor will nations, when they agree to
enter a League of Nations to prevent war.

As for the argument that war is necessary for
the development of virtue, this is surely the most
specious that could be imagined. For it is not
in war, but in peace, that war's heroes are
fashioned. Our V.C.'s were heroes before they
were proved on the battlefield, and they acquired
their splendid qualities in pursuing the arts of
peace, in the mills and offices in which they
worked, in the schools where they were taught,
and in the churches where they worshipped.
War only gave them a stage upon which to
display these qualities ; it was not their source or
origin. For one hero that the war has dis-
covered to us it has destroyed a thousand—nay,
tens of thousands—without discovering them.
For one who has had a chance of proving
himself in personal combat with the foe,
thousands have simply been swept away without

seeing the hand that destroyed them, and without the slightest opportunity of heroism. To-day valour counts less in war than shells and munitions and the accumulation of material resources. Will those who uphold war as a field for heroism dare to be logical and contend that it was either necessary or desirable that millions of men should be slaughtered in order to keep alive the sense of heroism in humanity? Will they hazard the absurdity that mankind is better for the example of our heroes than it would have been if their precious lives had been spared? Is their moral sense so depraved that, like spectators at the arena, they must see slaughter to restore their zest in life and their faith in humanity? And if they dare not plead these things, is not their whole argument, when offered as a defence or even an excuse for war, a rather contemptible subterfuge?

In reply to such critics, then, I would vary the words used by Lord Morley on a celebrated occasion : ''Our hopes are better than your fears.''

Even if the whole body of such objections were established they would not constitute so formidable an indictment as could be urged against perpetuation of the present system. Our choice lies, not between absolute right and absolute wrong, but rather between the risks of a great experiment in international government, to which the nations are urged by conscience and self-interest, and the infinitely greater risks of a return to the discredited balance of power. Belief in the practicability of a League may be largely a matter of faith, but not, I hasten to add, of unreasoning faith which refuses to face facts and shuts its eyes to difficulties, but rather of one which holds, without wavering, that the trials and sufferings endured by the nations in this war, and the new lessons they have learnt, have created an almost universal desire and a favourable atmosphere for an organization to prevent future wars. Humanity's self-preservation, as much as every claim of conscience, force us to this task. Every conceivable motive directs the nations to seek security, which they can only get by guaranteeing the security of others. They must reduce the occasions of war or face the prospect of another world-wide catastrophe that would wreck civilization.

And this widespread desire cannot be dismissed as a pious hope or a worthless artificiality, for, rightly regarded, it is as much a manifestation of the laws of moral growth as ever arose in the affairs of mankind. A movement arising in the hearts of millions of people of all races and languages cannot be described as against nature, or as something fantastic and unreal. On the contrary, it is as real and living as anything one can see or touch. It is a dominant aspiration stirring men's hearts, it is a moral force that compels recognition, it is, in concrete form, the grand object for which tens of thousands have given their lives in this war. If this be admitted, how can we think that the attempt—even before it has been made—to translate this mighty faith and impulse into the terms of a practical scheme must be against nature ? How can we say that it is a defiance of the established and inevitable necessities of life ?   How can we agree with Bernhardi that "the whole idea (of international government) represents a presumptuous encroachment on the natural laws of development "?   Is there a greater necessity written across the face of the world to-day than the necessity to make an end of war, or a more palpable development than the determination of nations to achieve this aim ? And if we were to say that any attempt to meet this necessity by practical measures must be foredoomed to failure as a violation of the laws of nature, should we not deny man every semblance of the power of self-determination ? Should we not make him the sport of chance ? Surely no conception of nature can be valid which excludes man's volitional activity and his development in society?   He is not a mere creature of circumstance, but the most conscious of all the forces of life, and his moral life has become, in the course of evolution, as much a part of nature as the appetites of the lower animals.

" . . . Nature is made better by no mean,
But Nature makes that mean ; over that art
Which you say adds to Nature is an art
That Nature makes."

If the demand for a League to protect the
world from war were cherished by only a few
politicians, it might be said to lack the force of
nature, but it is notorious that every living
spring of public opinion is pressing for it with
an insistence that politicians have not yet been
able to satisfy.

One may, however, admit as a danger what
one must resist as an objection. Any League
of Nations that is to be permanent must conform
to the laws of growth. It must provide for
change as well as stability. The mechanism
necessary to the discharge of its functions must
not be allowed to destroy its spirit. It must
allow for the expansion and contraction of
interests and provide for changes based on such
considerations. The attempt, at the outset,
to produce an absolute formula, or a too
elaborate cut-and-dried scheme, may prove

fatal. We should aim, as Lord Parker
advised, not at theoretic perfection, but rather
at the creation of a nucleus capable of expansion in the light of further needs and experience. We must not overcrowd the lifeboat.
But does not all experience show that half the
objections that are urged against great political
schemes disappear in practice ?   Many of them
arise through an attempt to anticipate every
remote contingency.   But, again, experience
shows that if a man accepts a body of principles
and is pledged in good will to maintain them,
he may be left free to a large extent to conform
his life and affairs to them. And a similar
result would probably follow the decision of a
state to enter a League of Nations.

Take the cost of armaments, for instance,
and the suggested creation of an international
force.   The whole aspect of this question would
be changed when the nations found that power
could not be derived from independent armaments, when every motive of self-interest
prompted in the contrary direction, and when

great advantage and security were offered by adherence to and dependence on a League. When armaments cease to pay it will not be necessary to proscribe them. No nation, even in ordinary times, would squander millions on weapons which had ceased to have any value as a means of aggrandisement or as a precautionary measure of defence. And after this war no nation will be in a position to maintain its pre-war standard of expenditure on armaments, on the top of the colossal burden of war debts which all have incurred.

It may be assumed, I think, that one of the conditions of membership of the League will be that every member shall abolish conscription as an unnecessary defensive precaution. For why should a Power wish to maintain conscription, unless it were bent on aggression, when its security would be guaranteed by the whole of the armed forces of the League? If ten Powers were each to limit themselves to an army of 100,000 volunteers, there would be a League army of a million men available in an emergency ; and if any attempt by a member to increase its military strength, without the authority of the League, were treated as a hostile act, how could it be possible for an aggressor to raise his head ? How, for instance, could a Power that had limited its armed forces to 100,000 men defy a group of Powers with an army of 900,000 men ? The latter could blockade the recalcitrant Power, cut it off from the world, exclude its exports, and refuse to send imports. Supposing Germany had been confronted with such a situation before the war, who can believe that she would have drawn the sword ? It is more reasonable to suppose that she would not have wasted her resources in a vain endeavour, any more than an individual would waste his strength in declaring war on the collective forces of society. No state is self-sufficing. Germany was dependent for her prosperity on the Allies before the war. Her trade with them was far greater than her trade with Austria, and it was this consideration which caused her to abandon the Mittel-Europa scheme as utterly impracticable. So far as she is concerned no one need fear the creation of a counter-league. She could not remain hostile to a League of which Britain, France, and America were members, and continue to live economically. Ten years of such conditions would reduce her to the level of a fourth-rate Power. Nothing is more obvious, I think, than that if any of the published schemes for a League of Nations were adopted nations would be infinitely more dependent upon one another than individuals are. Furthermore, it is not the hangman's rope, but moral repugnance that deters most men from murder ; and similarly, under a League of Nations, although penalties would be necessary, they would in course of time cease to be the chief deterrents. Whether or not a state has the attributes of moral personality, it must be governed even in an imperfect world very largely by moral principles. We cannot allow that it exists for itself, and is, in the ultimate resort, a corporation of pirates. The Germans conceive it as apart from and inde-

pendent of the community, whereas the only
admissible conception amongst civilized Powers
is that it is nothing more or less than "the community organized for political purposes."
Before the war the Kaiser more than once re-
peated the saying of Louis XIV., "L'état,
c'est moi," and it is this pernicious theory of the
irresponsibility of the state, and not a legitimate
law of growth, which the Allies are determined to
destroy once and for all. Surely nothing is
more obvious than that where a state is governed
by autocrats it takes its character from them,
and similarly, where it is governed by men who
recognize the claims of humanity and the obligations of Treaties, it rises to a higher level than
that of an abysmal selfishness. Even in this
war we have abundant evidence that States
which derive their authority from the community, and not from abstract conceptions of
power, are capable of disinterested sacrifices,
and recognize higher obligations than those that
arise from their material interests. Neither
Britain nor America went into this war from

selfish motives ; they were not concerned about self-preservation or material interests, but about the maintenance of certain cherished principles. They had committed themselves and the destiny of their peoples to those principles, and were resolved to defend them.

If a League were created, I venture to think that these moral and material deterrents would prove effective against most of the conceivable menaces that might arise. We cannot, in the nature of things, be assured of absolute security ; the best we can hope to achieve at present is to make war so difficult that it will occur less frequently, and may ultimately be eradicated.

II

"THE MANDATE OF HUMANITY"

II

"THE MANDATE OF HUMANITY"

By M. D. PETRE

I

" We are not obeying the mandate of parties or of politics, we are obeying a mandate of humanity."

THESE words of President Wilson, spoken at Manchester on December 30th, 1918, furnish a fitting text to this essay, which was mainly composed before they were uttered. The League of Nations is a mandate of humanity, not of politicians; the President of the United States is a spokesman of humanity, and not of party or politics. In this fact consists his strength, in this fact also will be found the explanation of his weakness, should he fail to achieve all that he has set before himself. He may prove too great, as a man, for his task as a politician; yet, even should this occur, his efforts will not be robbed of their fruit, for his position, as a statesman, will have obtained for him such a hearing as no private individual could obtain.

There are, as yet, few responsible statesmen who would venture to declare themselves definitely opposed to the scheme for a League of Nations, yet there are also, I will dare to say, few to whom it is a living and essential aim as it is to the great President. The very lack of vigorous criticism on the part of many is, to my mind, one great sign of their coldness ; and, in spite of the hopefulness engendered by the action of the Allied Conference, the lack of open opposition is not the best sign of earnestness.

The same may be said of the Press. After attending Viscount Grey's meeting, of October 10th, 1918, I was struck by the absence of Press criticism in quarters where the scheme is certainly not regarded with enthusiasm. Objections that appeared obvious were overlooked, while all that made for a reduced programme was set forth. My impression was thereby

deepened that wise adversaries do not exercise
the soundest criticism, because such criticism
is not favourable to their own ends. The
scheme will live or die in proportion to its power
of adjustment to the facts of life ; hence the
friendly critics are the friendliest friends. Many
adversaries of the scheme, having a keen sense
of its inherent impossibilities, are trusting to the
play of those impossiblities to reduce it eventually to what they regard as its suitable dimen-
sions.

I think, in fact, that the scheme is in need of
advocates in whom idealism is blended with a
strain of Machiavellism. By Machiavellism I
do not mean a doctrine of immoral expediency,
such as the term has unjustly come to signify.
By Machiavellism I mean the doctrine of
Machiavelli—the doctrine, namely, that statecraft is a science with its own object and laws,
and, like any other science, must be guided by
those laws. The science itself may be sub-
ordinate to other sciences that are higher and
wider in their scope ; it may, eventually, be

modified and widened by those nobler sciences ;
yet, so far as it goes, it cannot, without peril,
neglect its own laws.

Now President Wilson has given us the right
word for the scheme we are considering ; it is
'' a mandate of humanity,'' it is not a device of
politicians.   Yet it is put forward as almost the
chief item of a political programme, and this is
the problem with which we are about to deal in
the following essay.   There are those who do
not desire a League of Nations, there are those
who do not believe in it as a scheme of practical
politics, and, again, there are those who both
wish for it and believe in it as politically practicable.   This last is the attitude set forth in
the former of these two essays.

But there is yet another view of the matter
which is to be suggested in the following pages.
The League of Nations may be regarded as
mainly an object of human, and not political,
aspiration, and as depending for its *complete*
accomplishment on the efforts of mankind at
large and not on those of the official guides of

state policy.   In such case politicians may do something towards the end in view, but they will not do all ; they will be finally the executors of the scheme, but will never be its initiators.   If this view were a correct one, then time might be saved and errors avoided by its recognition. State policy is doomed to failure if it follow rules essentially alien to its constitution ; yet it may be employed as a means where it would fail as an originating force.   Some kind of a League of Nations might emanate from the Peace Conference without its being such as to satisfy the ideal that has been formed of it in the heart of the world at large.   This will not be a disappointment for those to whom statecraft is essentially limited in its aims ; yet neither will it be a reason for acquiescing in a mediocre fulfilment of human aspirations.   Where politicians end humanity can go on ; we need not be balked of our aim because our official rulers are unable to attain it for us.   Let us therefore face the political difficulties—I would almost call them contradictions—inherent in the scheme, without therefore wavering in our hope of its eventual fulfilment.

First, let us take a wholesome, though depressing, backward glance at history.

"*It was confidently expected,*" writes Dr. A. W. Ward, in the ninth volume of the Cambridge Modern History, "*that the distribution of the large mass of territories reconquered from France, and the resettlement of the political map of Europe, would proceed on principles ensuring a real and permanent equilibrium amongst its states, such as had not been established either at the close of the Thirty Years' War or that of the Spanish Succession. But more than this. In many quarters the hope was cherished that after promptly solving this part of its task the great assembly would, without loss of time, enter upon an ulterior range of labours, equally important and, from a cosmopolitan point of view, more inspiring. It would assuredly safeguard the settlement of the political system of Europe by the institution of an effective and* *enduring international tribunal. Further, by way of attesting its sincere desire of putting an end to the constant recurrence of war, the Congress would at least attempt to apply the remedy of a systematic, though at first inevitably partial, disarmament. It would encourage the growth of representative institutions, by which Napoleon himself had endeavoured to appease resistance or to conciliate support. It would obey the dictates of humanity, already followed by Great Britain, by extinguishing the African slave-trade . . . and, conceivably, freedom of traffic might be secured on the ocean itself, though, to be sure, Great Britain, then still at war with the United States on behalf of her navigation laws, was not likely to modify them in favour of neutrals."**

The programme is almost identical with that which faces the Peace Congress to come.

The same writer tells us that what the Congress actually did achieve was : *"To restore a number of princes to the dominions formerly*

* *Op. cit.*, p. 578.

held by themselves or their dynasties, and to revive the independent existence of a number of states which had been subjected to an alien rule; to furnish fresh securities for the reorganized political system of Europe by instituting a federal union of the states of Germany, strengthening that of the cantons of Switzerland, and opening a prospect of constitutional life for a number of European peoples; to rescue a large and unfortunate section of humanity from the indefinite endurance of a cruel and wicked abuse; and to add not a few further provisions favourable to the principle of tolerance, and to that of freer and more frequent intercourse between the nations."*

"But, on the other hand, no proposal for instituting a permanent tribunal of arbitration, or any similar authority for the settling of disputes between the states of Europe, could at present be expected to find serious support; the principles of the public Law of Nations, as interpreted by a preponderance of learning, had in

* *Idem*, p. 671.

the last resort to be enforced by the joint action of what Metternich called the 'moral Pentarchy,' approved and supported by the remaining Governments. When the Congress assembled, there were no doubt many hopes that the dawn of a long, if not perpetual, era of peace might itself be heralded by a general disarmament. The Congress gave no sign of the willingness of the European Governments, or of the Great Powers in particular, to entertain any such proposal."

The Congress, in fact, accomplished those things which the Great Powers, mainly constituting it, truly desired to accomplish, and could only accomplish in unison with one another ; but it did not accomplish those things which the Great Powers did not wholeheartedly desire to accomplish, nor those things which the Great Powers were wont and able to accomplish, not in unison with one another, but as separate forces and entities. Their aims were international only where nationality ended.

* *Idem*, p. 669.

The word *internationalism* is one that needs much close consideration. Does it mean such an intercourse of nations amongst each other as is fully compatible with the laws of national life and development? Or does it mean another and overruling system of political life, in which national claims are to be subordinated to other and higher ones? The distinction is an important one.

Viscount Grey compares the nation to the individual, and while admitting that such analogy is not perfect, he nevertheless points out that *individuals in civilized states have long ago accepted limitation and obligation as regards disputes between individuals; these are settled by law, and any individual who, instead of appealing to law, resorts to force to give effect to what he considers his rights, finds himself at once opposed and restrained by the force of the state—that is, in democratic countries, by the combined force of the other individuals.*

The analogy is, to my mind, so "imperfect"

as to be useless. The individual who resists the law finds himself up against the very world in which he has to live, of which he forms a part, on which he depends for the satisfaction of every need of mind and heart and body. Isolated from the rest, his resistance would be in vain ; and even if he should succeed in drawing a few other units to his side, their help would be utterly inadequate against the forces of the whole community. Even were the theory of the "Contrat Social," as the origin of society, literally true, the individual has by now—*qua* individual—so completely abdicated any separate means he ever possessed of enforcing his own will that not the highest mental qualifications, nor the greatest moral determination, nor the most violent passions, can recover them for him. He is helpless as against society, because he is a part of it. He may succeed in infecting society with some of his own microbes, and thus attain his aim through his influence on the rest of the community ; but *separately* he can do nothing.

Do not let us cherish any illusions in this
matter.   We may have the profoundest respect
for law and order ; we may know that our individual happiness and value depend on our own
acceptance of social authority ; yet our con-
scientious convictions in this matter do not
constitute the sole ground for our obedience.
It is the powerlessness of the individual, and
not his conviction of the necessity of law and
order, that constitutes the most unfailing and
persistent motive for obedience and submission.
Can we deny that there are many men and
women who if able, for good or evil, to do as
they thought right or wished to do, in despite
of society, would not do it ?   The good man
would resist society, as he believed, for its own
benefit ; the bad man would resist it for his own
pleasure.   It is because men cannot succeed
against the collective forces of society that they
do not waste time in a vain endeavour ; and
though most of us are conscious of the advantage of this helplessness—even as regards our
individual welfare—yet it is the fact of our help-

lessness, and not our reasoned acceptance of it, that will often constitute the chief ground of our obedience. Even Socrates, in his refusal to save his life at the expense of the law, was inspired not only by his love for the laws of his land, but by his sense of complete dependence on them. He, indeed, was of the stuff of which martyrs are made ; he died voluntarily and for an ideal. Yet the law, for him too, was not only holy, it was also potent.

Now compare the position of an individual in regard to the political community to which he belongs with the position of an individual nation in regard to the International Society which the League of Nations would constitute. The League of Nations, as hitherto conceived, would be the outcome of state-made treaties and conventions — an artificially fashioned system. Membership would be a matter of consent, not of necessity. There would be advantages attached to such membership, but if any nation found itself strong enough to secure more than those advantages by a breach of the laws of membership, such sanction would be destroyed. If the world had reached a stage in which each nation was as dependent on the goodwill of international society as each individual is dependent on the goodwill of the political society to which he belongs, there would be no talk of a League of Nations, because there would be no need for it.

We can regulate life, but only in obedience to its laws; and great as is the inspiring and creative force of ideas, we cannot artificially refashion the world in accordance with them. They must grow into the stuff of life, as religions have done, if they are to mould and recreate it. Religions have never been made. They have come from above, or they have grown, according as the supernatural or naturalistic interpretation of them be adopted. Comte tried to make a religion, and how much came of it ? though his philosophy has inspired the religion of many minds since his time.

So, too, social transformations are not wrought by conscious effort, or deliberate

measures, nor by the direct teaching of any
mind or minds. Rousseau may have had a
good deal to say to the French Revolution, but
it was the forces of the Revolution, not his
writings, that wrought the change. The
League of Nations supposes a new set of living
instincts and motives ; the nations that adopt it
must have a new political religion—and religion
cannot be made. I honestly doubt whether it
be in the nature of any living force to abandon
the regulation of its destiny to another in those
matters which it is able to decide for itself ; and
for a nation it is certainly less possible than for
an individual. Even if we adopt to the fullest
that philosophy which treats of the state as of a
moral personality, yet, even so, moral interests
are sufficiently complex, and selfish instincts are
sufficiently strong, to allow of any nation believ-
ing itself to be in the right against all the world.

Furthermore, in so far as states are endowed
with moral personality, they must also be
endowed with soul, and if with soul, then also
with conscience.

But of all things that cannot be shared between two or many, that are strictly personal and private and individual, the conscience is first and pre-eminent. In the last resort conscience will make its voice heard in despite of rule, in despite of force, in despite of numbers. In obedience to conscience men have broken law and defied Governments. In so far as a state has a conscience a state will do the same.

Now the conscience of a state cannot be ruled by those purely spiritual considerations which may sway the action of individuals; it stands too largely for material interests. It must, inevitably, be a coarser, more mundane conscience than that of the saint or prophet or reformer, yet a conscience it will be for all that; and when that conscience declares "this is wrong in relation to the ends for which I exist," whatever be the matter in dispute, be it a matter of material or of moral import, that conscience ought to prevail.

The state will progress as humanity progresses ; it will have a more directly moral end as the people which compose it rise to a higher moral level. But its main duties are, as yet, material rather than moral ; it protects the well-being of its children that they may work out their own spiritual salvation.

The conscience of a state cannot, therefore, be as delicate, as disinterested, as altruistic, as that of the noblest individuals. The state exists primarily for its own people and only secondarily for the rest of the world. Hence, given a dispute in which it feels its rights and welfare to be at stake, it may, however erroneously, set aside its moral obligations to international society in favour of its obligations to the people for whom it exists.

But no righteous conscience, it may be said, could give its verdict against a solemn pledge taken and reciprocated ; no righteous conscience could, in a society of nations, declare against the ends of that society. Indeed I think it could, and sometimes would, if its sense of justice were outraged ; if its duty to those who were bone of its bone and flesh of its flesh came into conflict with its duty to those not directly belonging to it.

Yet these cases might be rare, and might little interfere with the scheme we are discussing. I grant it, yet I urge the objection because it presents one more difficulty, and one more proof that our League is not quite in accordance with the law of nature. Conscience is our moral guide, but do not let us suppose therefore that its character is purely altruistic. It will sometimes lay down a law of self-sacrifice, but it will also lay down the rightful laws of self-preservation. The mechanism of a state exists mainly for its own preservation, and cannot be turned against this, its legitimate end. The conscience of a state will not traverse this main condition, and to weaken its conscience is to weaken its life.

An individual who finds himself in such a position is controlled by the law of necessity as well as moral considerations. Even if his conscience defy the world, he himself cannot do so ; he submits, habitually, not only because he ought, but also because he must. A state in the League of Nations will, unless some potent form of sanction be devised, be expected to submit only because it ought.

Thus do certain presentments of this scheme seem to me to come up against vital instincts, and to demand of nations that for which they will not be fitted until they no longer exist in the present sense of the word. The strong will not give way to the weak ; the one who thinks himself in the right will not yield to those whom he believes to be in the wrong ; the living generation will not be restrained by the promises of a dead one ; nature will not be controlled by conventions.

It will here be urged that this necessity has been fully recognized, and that one great problem of the scheme is the devising of some form of sanction—that is to say, of punishment for those who err. Let us pass, then, to a consideration of the methods proposed.

The League of Nations Society declares that the states *that are members of that Society shall jointly use forthwith both their economic and military forces against any one of their number that goes to war.*

Viscount Grey, in his speech of October 10th, said even more than this. He suggested that the League of Nations might exercise a kind of universal police duty.

"*I do not see,*" he said, "*why it should not arrange for an authority, and an international force at its disposal, which should act as police act in individual countries.*"

He adduces certain cases in which such interference might be useful, and again says :

"*I think these cases might be settled, if force be necessary, by a League of Nations, if it had an international force at its disposal.*"

I quote his very words, because otherwise I might seem to be suggesting a difficulty that does not exist. What else can he mean but the formation of a collective international army ?

Certainly strange things come true, and I may be as mistaken as others are right, but this notion does strike me as one of the strangest and most unpractical political conceptions that have ever been enounced. Elsewhere I gave what seemed to me an example of such a policy.

*" In the great Schism of the West there were two rival Popes. An unfortunate effort was made to end the trouble by electing a third and deposing the other two. Unfortunately the other two declined to be deposed, and thus the Church was left with three rivals instead of two."**

I have not yet been able to move from the conviction which I there set forth.

Of what is this "international force" to consist? where is it to be located? under what immediate authority is it to act? Is it to have a huge international barracks of its own, with a staff and generals and equipment? or is each section to be lodged and commanded in the land from which its forces are drawn? The difficulties against either alternative are overwhelming.

* "Reflections of a Non-Combatant" (Longmans and Co.).

As to the first, such a force, to be efficient, must be immense ; hence our first move towards universal peace would be the setting up of a peculiarly gigantic army.   If such army were lodged on neutral territory the whole world would be at its mercy should it become corrupt.

Again, our international army would have, almost perforce, to be composed of a professional soldiery, and even the much misunderstood Machiavelli declared that a professional soldiery—which was in his days, and would be in the case before us, a purely mercenary soldiery—is "scandalous, idle, undisciplined, irreligious."   Are we to take such a step backwards in our effort to secure peace ?   Again, how are we to count on the loyalty of any national section of our army when it is called on to act against its own country ?   And one disloyal section may carry many others with it.

If we suppose the second alternative, then other difficulties present themselves.   If each state keeps a section of the international force on its own territory, how are we to expect that a naughty member of the League will not at once divert such force, by persuasion or compulsion, to its own ends ?   And, obviously, the larger sections of our international force will be lodged by the larger nations adhering to the League ; hence the stronger the dissident the greater the danger.

So much as regards a concrete international force.

But another method might be conceived. Without maintaining any common army each member of the League might pledge itself to employ its own forces when called upon to do so by the general Tribunal or Council of the League.   Here, again, there are surely grave questions to be answered.   Once more it is obvious that the strongest nations will have the largest forces at their disposal, and that, consequently, if the naughty one be also a strong one, as will almost always be the case, we shall at once find a powerful rebel to deal with, and a rebel that will probably have made underground preparations before venturing into the open.

Furthermore, how are we to expect that any
rebellious member will not both seek and gain
adherents amongst its neighbours, especially
the weaker ones ?   Either by persuasion, or by
force, it will draw others in its wake ; and we
shall have the tragic spectacle of a great war
undertaken for the preservation of peace.

But there is another form of pressure which is
even more generally advocated, and that is
economic pressure.   Will this, exercised simply
as a punitive measure, be more efficient than
the military safeguard ?   With the secession of
any nation from the League her pledges are
broken, and she will at once set about to take,
by force or by fraud, what is not conceded to
her in other ways.   A strong rebel will feed
and warm herself at the stores of her weaker
neighbours, and will promptly dislocate all
international arrangements.   She may suffer
for it in the end, but also she may not, until
much disaster has been caused by her resistance.   The fact is that the safeguards hitherto
suggested all depend on the general loyalty for

their efficiency, and are liable to break down just when they are needed. Once more, then, I would urge my point, that the obedience of each nation will only be secured in proportion to its dependence, and that the League must in some way ensure this dependence if it is to be safe and solid. That such dependence of each one on the welfare of all may eventually be secured is indeed a great possibility, but I cannot see that the measures hitherto suggested are likely to be adequate. If we are to form a great human family, we must aim at such a community of interests as will render prohibitory laws acceptable to its members.

Viscount Grey says in his pamphlet :

"The idea must be adopted with earnestness and conviction by the Executive Heads of States. It must become an essential part of their practical policy, one of their chief reasons for being or continuing to be responsible for the policy of their states."

This is the ordinary view of those who hold to the scheme, but it is, of course, the very

question as to which dispute is raised in this
essay.   Can a scheme of this magnitude, so
vastly human in its aims, depend wholly, even
for its political advancement, on the goodwill
and exertions of professional politicians ?

The war has had one curious effect on the
general mind in giving a hitherto inexperienced
sense of being governed.   Of course we always
knew we had a Government—it kept things
going ; it managed our foreign affairs ; it dealt
with labour questions ; it maintained, and sometimes modified, the English Constitution.   All
this was of interest to us as British citizens, but
we had not, nevertheless, any distinct experience of a personal relationship, as the governed,
to the official class of rulers.

But now we have.   We are daily conscious
of interference with our personal liberty and
inclinations ; we are subjects of the state in a
more directly practical manner than before.
The result has been, I think, a disposition to
more pungent criticism of our legislators than
was formerly exercised.   Our morning news-

paper is not a matter of mere academic discussion, it rouses questions in which we take an active personal interest.

Now I think a consequence of this change must be, in the minds of intelligent people, along with a sense of our direct dependence on the Government under which we live, a sense of their inevitable weakness and inadequacy in dealing with the great forces of human life ; but, on the other hand, this spirit of criticism is modified by a sense of our own incompetence to sit in judgment on their conduct while we remain in such total ignorance of a large proportion of the facts with which they have to deal. We feel ourselves, therefore, in a conflicting temper of mind ; we do not always trust our rulers to do what is wisest and best, yet neither do we trust ourselves to know what ought to be done, or, still more, what can be done. The ropes are in their hands, not in ours ; yet we are not quite sure that they will handle those ropes in such a manner as to guide the ship in the direction whither the best aspirations of the world would convey her. Our rulers tell us, more often than we believe their statements, that they are our mandatories ; yet we half think that a good many of our aims and ideals are quietly shelved when they sit down to manage our affairs. Perhaps this is because we are asking for the impossible, and until we know more of what is going on behind the scenes we cannot be sure that they are not right in telling us so ; but perhaps, on the other hand, what we ask is not impossible, and it is only their laws of precedent, and the habits of their office, that make them think it so.

It happens to me, from time to time, to find myself discussing public affairs with one of the official world, when I have practical experience of what I have just said. I feel, in the first place, that he knows exactly what he is talking about, and that I only know about half. I feel, in the second place, that my notions may be wildly impracticable, given certain facts, conventions, treaties, information, of which he has knowledge, and of which I am ignorant.

And yet, though I really am not one given to talking of things I don't understand, I talk on, and my justification, if I have one, is this—namely, that I think the official class understand the mechanism of their own job, but do not understand how far that job itself is dependent on wider human facts ; that I think they are bound, eventually, to find place for ideas which they can still afford to ignore ; that their perceptions are blinded by precedent, and their power of initiative overlaid by habit and routine. Furthermore, I know that they are subjected to a very definite code of discretion and very clearly appointed rules of speech.

All this points, as Mr. E. D. Morel would tell us, to the evils of secret diplomacy. I don't want to embark on that question, but whatever the rights and wrongs of it may be, this much at least seems to me obvious—namely, that, by the secret methods of the official politician, the wider aspirations of humanity will never be realized.

As I have said elsewhere, "*Europe has made*

many treaties, but she has never yet made peace,''* nor will she ever do so at the hands of diplomats or rulers. Why? Because their power and their ability, their traditions and their training, do not go beyond the making of treaties. A treaty is an arrangement, having for its aims the granting and obtaining of certain advantages ; it rests partly on the honour of the treating parties, but still more on their needs and interests. A treaty is made up of material pledges and promises ; an honourable state will abide by those promises unless, or until, higher or more imperative considerations force it to repudiate them. For that they can, under certain circumstances, be repudiated, without moral disgrace, is surely obvious, otherwise how could war ever arise at all ?

A treaty, then, is what I should call an artificial production ; it is a thing made, not grown ; it embodies the claims and necessities of the contracting parties, not their temper and dispositions. A treaty drawn up at the close of

* " Reflections of a Non-Combatant."

hostilities stands for the cessation of a war, and not for the inauguration of a peace.

Peace, on the other hand, is not a convention, but a condition of mind and soul ; it is not a composition of rivalries, but a stilling and effacement of them ; it is not a compromise, but a harmony ; it is not a computation of conflicting claims, an adjustment of conflicting interests, but a dissolution of conflict into union, of rival claims into co-operation. This is a work beyond the range of diplomatic endeavour ; it is a social and not a political task ; politicians will be able to carry it out when society has prepared the way. Politicians are not inhuman, but it is the machinery of life, and not life itself, with which they are concerned.

I feel then that I am not so wholly foolish as I must appear when I discuss public affairs with ''one who knows.'' He knows what can be done in his own domain, he does not know how far that domain may be modified by the bigger world for which it exists. He knows how to do what I want done ; I know what I want done ;

and in so far as I want what the best of the world wants, he will have some day to do it.

A friend said to me a little while ago that, on the whole, the political cynicism of the ruling class was wholesome and beneficial. In its atmosphere unpractical idealism is checked and its dangers eliminated.

There is much truth and common sense in the observation ; politics are a science, with the limitations of a science. The saint, the prophet, the reformer, are amongst us to express the best of which mankind is capable, and to lead us on to its fulfilment ; they are not always those who can point to the means as well as to the end.

What I would ask is a much fuller recognition of the limitations of officialism ; a greater readiness, on the part of those who act for us all, to recognize that they have to do, with knowledge and science, those things which humanity desires with love and passion. The League of Nations, as expressive of world-wide aspirations, is not the conception of politicians ; nor will it be their achievement save in so far as humanity presses them on to its fulfilment. In their hands alone it would become an alliance, and not a human brotherhood. For this we should be wrong to blame them, because they have, in fact, to consider the duties of their own job. Indeed, one wishes sometimes that the cynicism of which my friend spoke were rather more generally recognized. Some minds are weary of the cant which has been talked during the course of the war, and I think it could have been avoided by distinguishing between political necessities and human ideals. We want some things because we are men, and all men are our brethren ; we want other things because we are Englishmen, or Frenchmen, and England or France is our country. I don't want to be always saying that my country is in the right— I'd stand by her even if she were in the wrong ; and though I think our cause is a just one, I don't believe in all these big professions of disinterestedness. One great disadvantage of someone being egregiously in the wrong is that all the rest of us are inclined to think ourselves egregiously in the right. I do not think that the duty of self-criticism is discharged by an indictment of the crimes of Germany. We talk of our ideals until we forget that we have other, and more selfish, aims as well. I don't think our idealism would be lessened by greater sincerity, nor that we should do less for others by admitting that we wanted also to get something for ourselves.

International morality is in the making ; it is not yet fully made, and perhaps by the time it has come into its own the expression will no longer be suited to the thing. So long as separate states exist the claims of self-regard may conflict with those of international disinterestedness ; and if ever a World-State supersede all other states, the term "international" will lose its meaning. At present such an end is too remote to guide our immediate efforts ; and it seems to me, therefore, a misdirection of energy to suppose moral excellences that are not in accordance with life as it now exists.

II

The difficulties that have been presented in the foregoing pages may be resumed as follows :

1. A League of Nations must not rely, for its preservation, on military or economic coercion.

2. It must not override the claims—even the more selfish and materialistic claims—of state and nation ; it must not ignore that primary instinct in virtue of which all living things exercise their right and their might in the work of self-defence and self-development and do for themselves what they are able to do. This instinct can be modified, but not suppressed.

3. An official class has, in the first place, official duties ; politicians are more imbued with political science than with human idealism ; a statesman thinks primarily of the state, even if he does not think primarily of his party, and the human heart has higher aspirations than the politician is ready to fulfil.

4. The success of the League will not depend on its police precautions, but on the mutual dependence which it promotes amongst the states that compose it. They must be as members of one family if family authority is to be respected.

5. And yet, though the scheme is human rather than political in character, it must not evolve into a league of inexperts against experts ; the fortunes of the state must not be risked by the action of even the best men who are no statesmen.

We have, then, a certain number of states seeking to enter into some sort of union with one another, but each one jealous of its own independence, each one conscious of its own power of self-defence and self-determination, each one with a soul of its own and a conscience corresponding to that soul.

Suppose some supreme Parliament composed of representatives of these nations—what binding force can the decisions of such a parliament be hoped to possess ? How far will even promises, made in the past, avail in a world of ever-changing conditions ?

As Mr. Zimmern has so truly said, in his discussion of the " International Council " proposed by the Union of Democratic Control :

" *If this suggestion is intended to be practicable, it presumably means an inter-state council—that is to say, a council composed of nominees from all the states, or all the leading states, of the world. . . . But the real crux of the formula lies in the moral 'decisions.' In what sense is this council going to decide things? . . . Are they going to be an assembly of envoys or an assembly of representatives— in other words, a Parliament?   If the former, I welcome the suggestion. . . .   But I see in such a suggestion no 'guarantee of an abiding peace.' . . .   An international council can only be effective as an organ of government if it is part of a World-Government acting according to a regular written constitution; and such a constitution could only be set going after it had been adopted by a convention representa-*

*tive of all peoples or governments concerned. Before the suggested council could have authority to decide things . . . Frenchmen, Germans, Turks, Russians, and citizens of other existing states must have declared their willingness to merge their statehood in a larger whole and to hand over their forces, or the greater part of them, to the new central government. This may be what the formula means. It may be intended to allow a government of Germans, Magyars, Russians, Turks, or any other chance majority to use the British and French navies to carry out its purposes. If this is meant it should be said."**

— It has always seemed to me that the doctrine of individual selfishness can only be combated, *non-morally*, by the law of expediency, by the fact that pure selfishness does not pay ; or *morally* by the law of solidarity, by the belief that we are all rooted in one great whole, whose welfare is the welfare of all. Pure altruism is a fiction ; I mean the love of another in place

* "Nationality and Government," pp. 41-43.

of the love of self. The League of Nations will only become a reality in proportion as such solidarity comes to exist between states as now exists between individuals and the community. The world is not yet ripe for complete international solidarity, but a League of Nations signifies nothing at all unless it means a move in that direction. How is such solidarity to be promoted? Very little by force; very little by treaties; very much by the pursuit of common objects, the sharing of common interests, and the establishment of such an international system of co-operation as will render each state dependent on the welfare of the rest. Submission to international law will be in proportion to dependence on international ends; nations must share a family board before they accept a family authority.

We will not enter into fiscal questions. We will not discuss the subject of free trade, though it would certainly seem that every open market, every open port, every open sea, must contribute to the success of a League of Nations.

But, at long last, we must look to something more than statecraft for the promotion of our object; and though the actual League of Nations, if it come into concrete being, must be the work of statesmen and not of unqualified workers or thinkers, yet these latter may have to do a great deal which the former will not do for them, and I cannot but think it possible that on unofficial workers will fall much of the real initiation of the scheme.

I have always felt that one of the chief excellences of the British Constitution is not what it does for us, but what it allows us to do for ourselves.   In the course of history many great moves have been effected by the primary action of unofficial organizations.   When these organizations work in despite of the existing government, we have some form of revolution ; when they act on it, we have constitutional reforms or changes.   I think the example of Russia has made us all rather shy of revolutionary methods, even if they were not wholly unsuccessful in a country with the power of readjustment that France possesses, and that, on the whole, the form of constitutional pressure is the more potent and far reaching. Every state is nourished by the human beings that compose it, and what they truly will the state itself must eventually will, and this in proportion to the elasticity and democratic nature of its constitution. Much time may be wasted in expecting of the state things which the state is not qualified to perform ; still more time may be wasted, and more grievous loss incurred, by setting up ideas against facts, by using state machinery for ends to which it is not fitted. Officialism, whether political or ecclesiastical, is blind and heavy and imperceptive ; so is a steam-plough, so is a threshing-machine, but both are admirably suited to the prosecution of our ends.

I think, therefore, that the Peace Congress, to which we are looking for the fulfilment of so many ideals, will have a great deal to do besides fulfilling them ; that it will display some of the characteristics of the Congress of Vienna in the

conflict that must arise between materialistic
and spiritual views of life. It is true that the
League of Nations has been made into a definite
feature of the programme—the chief feature,
as President Wilson would have it. This is a
great matter, and what the results of it may be
one cannot predict. The success of the idea,
even as carried out by professional statesmen,
may far outrun one's hopes and almost fulfil
one's wishes. Yet it is possible that the
difficulties may be too great for immediate
solution, and that the scheme, while not abandoned, may fall far short of its true ideal. It may
bear the mark of its time, a time of war and conflict ; it may be, it probably will be, a political
rather than a human achievement.

Viscount Grey said, in his speech, that
hitherto we have had the locomotive without
the steam—as, for example, in the Hague
Tribunal—while in the League of Nations we
shall have the machinery with the steam. Yet
I asked myself, as I listened to him, in what the
steam would consist, and whether it would not

be exactly on this point that international effort would once more prove futile. At the Vienna Congress those who were not dancing were so busy with territorial rearrangements that little time was left for the wider aims that were to be discussed.

Why, then, should nothing be done independently of official statedom—independently, I say, not in opposition to it? More and more does it seem as though parliamentary government were becoming executive rather than deliberative. The measures with which it has to deal are prepared for it by other forces outside; its task is to say *yea* or *nay*; to limit or expand or modify those measures. Hitherto it is chiefly the labour class that has constituted the great outside controlling force; but it is surely time for other interests to act in like manner, to consolidate their action and bring it to bear on the governing mechanism, if they are to have their proper share in the work of society.

Mr. Zimmern rightly deprecates the notion

of an International Council of *representatives*,
such as the Union for Democratic Control
would seem to suggest—of *representatives* with
a power of decision.   Such a Council might be
useful, he holds, if formed of *envoys*, whose
object would be mutual enlightenment and discussion.   But I should like to go a step farther
than Mr. Zimmern, and suggest that those
envoys should not only have no power to bind
their respective Governments to any practical
decision, but that they should likewise have no
responsibility to their respective Governments,
but should be independent of them both in their
origin and their action.

Let our chosen leaders elaborate their scheme
for the League of Nations, but, meanwhile, let
all the great sections of society, in every land,
form their own International Council—a
Council on which labour and capital, intellect
and industry, art and science, ethics and
religion, should have their delegates.   In this
Council there would be no representation of
reigning Governments, whether such Govern-

ments were democratic or autocratic, whether the Head of the state were a President Wilson or a Kaiser Wilhelm. They would bear no mandate from their rulers; they would carry no responsibility in their regard; they would pledge them to nothing.

But what use would there be in mere discussion? What value in votes deprived of all executive force?

As to the votes, let me wait awhile before saying what I want to say in the matter. As to the value of discussion, there would, first of all, be the advantage which Mr. Zimmern admits:

*"The more discussion and interchange and sifting of views we can have between public men in different states the better."**

But there would be a much more definite and practical advantage than this in such a Council as I would see established. For these envoys would not content themselves with mere discussion; their discussions would, when fruitful

* " Nationality and Government," p. 42.

and unanimous, issue in *resolutions*, and it would
be those *resolutions* that would make of the
International Council a potent factor of political
evolution.

Say that our members agreed on some international measure, they could not, themselves,
put it into force ; they could not pledge their
Governments to do so ; but they could pledge
themselves to undertake every lawful means to
bring about its fulfilment.   The members, as
mandatories of different interests in their own
land, would act through those interests on the
Government under which they lived.   A resolution of the International Council would signify,
for its members, an obligation to employ their
abilities, and all the influence they possessed,
whether by their votes or by other forms of
political action, to ensure the official acceptance
of that resolution.   Yet the envoys of each
country would find, in their respective Governments, the usual check that the politician offers
to any overstrained international idealism ; the
usual caution that a statesman exercises in his

dealings with other states. They would come in contact with the inert opposition of national egotism, and would be forced to recall the fact, if they had happened to forget it, that they were citizens of a state as well as members of an International Council. Yet our International Council might surely supply that steam which, as Viscount Grey truly said, has hitherto been lacking to the locomotive—a steam which does not seem to me easy of generation by state mechanism.

One great advantage of such a Council is that it needs the permission of no one for its formation, and that it would be the direct work of mankind at large. Yet it would be neither revolutionary nor alien in its character, for no member need be detached from his duty as citizen of his own land.

As to its methods of deliberation, I own I could wish it to depart from the voting tradition; at least from that of ballot voting. For this I have many reasons to give. First of all, such a Council should surely be as free as possible

8

from the entanglements of party system ; a system which votes tend to generate. The whole object of the Council would be enlightened and disinterested consideration of measures that tended to the common good, without running counter to the essential interests of each state. We should need something of that detachment which is so hardly combined with political interests. We may not always get it, even in our International Council ; but, even if we had it, the system of voting would weaken it.

Again, there seems to me no sense in making matters of truth and principle the subject of a vote. I have always thought this one great anomaly of an Œcumenical Council, for how can anything be proved true by the fact that the majority think it so ? The majority may be wrong and the minority right. Now our International Council would deal with principles as well as practical measures, and, for the same reason, would have no right to establish the truth in virtue of a mere numerical majority.

Lastly, I think the various delegates could

expect but little support in their own country when they came home to advocate a scheme that had only been accepted by a majority; nothing short of unanimity could win sufficient respect to overcome opposition. Very often even unanimity would not be sufficiently imposing to ensure the acceptance of measures in any way distasteful to national prejudice, but anything short of it would be quite ineffectual. We allow of nothing but unanimity in a court of law, and I think we could content ourselves with nothing less in an International Council.

I must repeat myself once more, and say that the obedience which so many seem to expect from states that enter the League is not, to my mind, easily obtainable. Viscount Grey says :

"*The second condition essential to the foundation and maintenance of a League of Nations is that the Governments and peoples of the states willing to found it understand clearly that it will impose some limitation upon the national action of each.*"

In so far as such limitation demands the actual subjection of a strong nation to the will of the rest, I do not believe we are ready for it ; and by the time, if ever, that we *are* ready for it, I fancy that the need for our League will have passed. As Mr. Zimmern says :

"*Two states are either sovereign, or they are united or federated; they cannot be half and half. A man must know of what state he is a citizen, and to what authority his duty is due. We all have our duty to render to Cæsar, but we cannot serve two Cæsars at once.*"*

But if the League of Nations cannot be founded on the *obedience* of those that compose it, it can very well be founded on their *dependence;* and the International Council could aim, above all, at measures tending to co-operation, and, through co-operation, to friendly interdependence. As to the question of disarmament, could it possibly be worked with less danger, less quarrels, less suspicion ?

And now there is another section of humanity

* "Nationality and Government," p. 44.

which must not be overlooked, and that is the Native Races.

In regard to this question, I own to a continued sense of exasperation when even professional politicians speak of these subject races as though we were about to grant them the same right of self-determination which we set forth as a part of our programme for European nationalities. What do we mean by it? Do we mean it for German colonies or for all? If for the former only, then it is not a question of self-determination for the natives, but of retribution for Germany; if for all, do we really understand what such a policy would signify?

Germany may be the worst master, but are any of us without fault? Some of us have a right to cast more stones than others, but we are all living in glass houses. These races have been subjected, in the first instance, by a course of brutal conquest; and have been exploited, in the second instance, chiefly for the ends of the conqueror, and only secondarily, if at all, for the good of the conquered. Some of us are trying to do better, none of us are doing quite well.

And yet it is surely but mischievous folly to endeavour to right the wrong by placing the savage in a position to choose for himself. It is not our domination that is wrong—such domination is in the law of nature, and even more necessary to the undeveloped races than it is profitable to us. It is the character of our sovereignty, and not that sovereignty in itself, that needs to be reformed.

Furthermore, the dignity of the white man is an essential element in his government of native races, and an appeal to them as to the choice of rulers would lessen their sense of awe and inevitableness. Even the introduction of native races into this great war, the importation of coloured troops to the Western front, must be regarded as a regrettable necessity—somewhat as though we had made a neighbour's children fight for us. Still more disastrous would it be to employ anything in the nature of cajolery or persuasion in our dealings with them. Those who understand children know how fatal are such methods in dealing with them; infant nations are similar in their requirements.

The retention, or non-retention, of German Colonies seems to me, therefore, a political and not a moral question; the moral obligation on all of us is to arrive at some concerted plan for the better treatment of those weaker races over which we must continue to rule.

I once suggested an "Inter-Colonial Native Council, to discuss and set forth native grievances and needs," which Council might "refer its decisions to a corresponding European Inter-Colonial Council, charged with the interests and protection of the native races."*

It seems to me that such a Native Inter-Colonial Council might be a fitting adjunct to the International Council we are discussing. This is a matter on which all are, at least in theory, agreed; it is therefore one on which we may surely hope for definite action and real reform. The notion of such an International

* The *New Statesman*, January 12, 1918.

Council may incur the favourite charge of
idealism. What matter, provided that idealism
be controlled by facts? The dangerous
idealism is that which asks that work shall be
done by the wrong workmen ; that soldiers shall
advocate disarmament and politicians altruism,
or even unadulterated Christianity. Let soldiers be asked to make war as decent as it can
be ; let politicians be asked to leave room for
the growth of human ideals. Let us use our
rulers and obey them, but not depend on them
for the satisfaction of all our highest aspirations.

I think, then, that we may co-operate with
and rejoice at every step towards the political
realization of a League of Nations ; but that,
should it disappoint our expectations, all is not
lost. The forces of humanity are wider and
deeper than those of political life ; statesmen
can only bring about the measures for which
mankind is prepared. The rivalries of separate
states and nations must be burnt up in the
furnace of human love before politicians can
dare to love their neighbours as themselves.

The time has come for a great move forward. Indeed, it would certainly appear as though the choice now lay between a leap—even a dangerous leap—into a new condition of things, or a reversion to the most extreme forms of militarism. Yet it is not men trained to the delicate technicalities of statecraft and diplomacy that will or ought to take such a leap. So long as we need their skill and labour—and we surely do yet need it—we have no right to blame them for not doing what would be a denial of their own character. But the world has a higher destiny than they can compass, and they will, at last, have the ability to achieve what humanity is bold enough to initiate and noble enough to desire.

BILLING AND SONS, LTD., PRINTERS, GUILDFORD, ENGLAND

A CATALOGUE *of* BOOKS
ON THE GREAT WAR
INCLUDING POPULAR HISTORIES OF ALL THE COUNTRIES AFFECTED BY IT, AND VOLUMES ON COMING RECONSTRUCTION PROBLEMS
Published by MR. T. FISHER UNWIN, London

ALSACE-LORRAINE: Past, Present and Future
By Coleman Phillipson, M.A., LL.D., Litt.D. Royal 8vo, cloth, 25/- net.

In this book the numerous matters and issues arising out of the question of Alsace-Lorraine are discussed analytically and critically with clearness, concision, and adequate fulness. Many delicate points involving conflicting claims are carefully examined in accordance with the dictates of right and logic.

TERMINATION OF WAR AND TREATIES OF PEACE
By Coleman Phillipson, M.A., LL.D., Litt.D., Barrister-at-Law. Royal 8vo, cloth, 21/- net.

"No systematic and comprehensive treatise on this subject, it would seem, at present exists ; and now that it is becoming one of urgent practical importance, the student and the man of affairs alike will welcome its full discussion by a leading authority on international law."—*The Times*.

LESSONS OF THE WORLD WAR
By Augustin Hamon, Professor at the Université Nouvelle of Brussels and at the Collège Libre des Sciences Sociales, Paris ; Lecturer at the London School of Economics and Political Science. Demy 8vo, cloth, 16/- net.

A penetrating, detached, and highly critical study of the causes of the Great War, and still more of its effects on the life of the nations engaged in it, and of the neutral peoples.

THROUGH EGYPT IN WAR TIME

By Captain Martin S. Briggs, A.R.I.B.A., author of of "Baroque Architecture." Profusely illustrated. Demy 8vo, cloth, 21/- net.

The contents include: In Cairo; Life on the Canal; The Oldest Road in the World; El Arish to Palestine; The Western Oases, etc., etc.

INTERNATIONAL LAW AND THE GREAT WAR

By Coleman Phillipson, M.A., LL.D., Litt.D. With an Introduction by Sir John Macdonell, K.C.B., LL.D. Demy 8vo, cloth, 15/- net.

"A valuable review by a leading authority both of the flagrant infractions of international law which have marked the present war, and of the changes caused by new conditions of war and industry which must inevitably take place in international law."—*The Times.*

THE INVASION AND THE WAR IN BELGIUM: From Liége to the Yser.

With a sketch of the diplomatic negotiations preceding the conflict. By Leon van der Essen, LL.D., Professor of History in the University of Louvain. With about 25 Maps and Plans. Demy 8vo, cloth, 15/- net.

"When, in a century or two, dispassionate historians endeavour to write the first act of the world war, they will find gathered in this work a store of valuable documents."—*Observer.*

THE ECONOMICS OF PROGRESS

By the Right Hon. J. M. Robertson, author of "The Future of Militarism," etc. Demy 8vo, cloth, 12/6 net.

Economic science, in Mr. Robertson's view, is a light to the path of social progress. Among the questions the book deals with in the light of economics are Education, Labour, Land and Capital, Commerce and Population.

THE FUTURE OF THE SOUTHERN SLAVS
By A. H. E. Taylor.   Demy 8vo, cloth, 12/6 net.

"The book is most exhaustive and comprehensive. . . No less remarkable than the author's grasp and knowledge of his subject is the force with which he argues the case for Serbia.   His book lets a flood of light upon the Balkans at the most opportune moment."—*National News.*

AUSTRALIA IN ARMS
A Narrative of the Australian Imperial Force and their achievement at Anzac.   By Phillip F. E. Schuler.   With 32 full-page Illustrations and Maps. Demy 8vo, cloth, 12/6 net.   [*Second Impression*

"Altogether the book is much the best of those we have seen which gives an account of the part taken by the Australians and New Zealanders in the eastern campaign." —*Saturday Review.*

"An important contribution to the historical literature of the war."—*Land and Water.*

THROUGH RUSSIA IN WAR TIME
By C. Fillingham Coxwell.   With 54 Illustrations. Demy 8vo, cloth, 12/6 net.

"A work based on personal travel, full of observation, well sifted, and with pleasant and useful illustrations."—*Daily Chronicle.*

"This is a book to be bought, borrowed, begged for, or stolen.   It is all so delightfully simple, interesting and *accurate.*"—*English Review.*

THE TURKISH EMPIRE: Its Growth and Decay
By Lord Eversley.   With a Frontispiece and Three Maps.   Demy 8vo, cloth, 12/6 net. [*Second Impression*

"Covers the whole history of Turkey from its first contact with Europe down to the Young Turk revolution, and shows the same gift of just and lucid narrative that made his history of Poland so valuable."—*Westminster Gazette.*

CHARLES LISTER: LETTERS AND RECOLLECTIONS

With a Memoir by his Father, Lord Ribblesdale. Demy 8vo, cloth, 12/6 net. [*Fifth Impression*

Charles Lister was one of that band of distinguished young men, including Rupert Brooke and Denis Browne, who went out with the Royal Naval Division to the Dardanelles. "It is a very bright and gallant and engaging personality that is presented to us in these pages."—*Observer*.

THE HISTORY OF TWELVE DAYS: July 24 to August 4, 1914

Being an Account of the Negotiations preceding the Outbreak of War, based on the Official Publications. By J. W. Headlam, M.A. Demy 8vo, cloth, 10/6 net.

"Mr. Headlam has written an exceptionally full, clear, and able analysis of the diplomatic negotiations during the twelve momentous days before Great Britain entered the war." —*The Times*.

BELGIANS UNDER THE GERMAN EAGLE

By Jean Massart. Demy 8vo, cloth, 10/6 net.

A very full and carefully documented account of what the Belgians have suffered under German rule.

"M. Massart's book will be regarded by posterity as a valuable historical document."—*Morning Post*.

FREEDOM IN FINANCE

By Oswald Stoll, author of "The People's Credit and the Grand Survival." Demy 8vo, cloth, 10/6 net.

This book deals with the power of credit in economics to reduce to dependence all individuals outside an inner ring. It formulates the means whereby credit might be widely distributed as a right, and incidentally it throws light on effects upon war policy and war finance resulting from the oligarchical principle of financial control which political authorities have been induced to support by the vicious economic fallacy of confusion between real money and credit.

KITCHENER IN HIS OWN WORDS

By J. B. Rye, formerly History Scholar of Balliol College, Oxford, and Horace G. Groser. Large Crown 8vo, cloth, 10/6 net.

"A full chronological record, which will be of much value for reference, of the events in Lord Kitchener's life, with selections from his utterances or writings, and some others bearing upon his work."—*The Times*.

ANZAC MEMORIAL

Edited by A. G. Stephens. Published for the Returned Soldiers Association of New South Wales. Illustrated. Demy 8vo, cloth, 10/6 net.

The "Anzac Memorial" volume includes original soldiers' stories of fighting at Gallipoli, and in Papua; the full text of General Hamilton's three despatches from the Dardanelles, and numerous illustrations and portraits.

MODERN AUSTRIA: Her Racial and Social Problems.

With a Study of ITALIA IRREDENTA. By Virginio Gayda. Translated by Z. M. Gibson and C. A. Miles. Demy 8vo, cloth, 10/6 net.

"The book is a treasure house. The discerning reader will set it with his Bryce and his Trevelyan. It clears up dozens of points upon which we would wish to inform ourselves."—*Daily Graphic*.

RUSSIA AND EUROPE

By Gregor Alexinsky, author of "Modern Russia," etc. Demy 8vo, cloth, 10/6 net.

"The book will be invaluable to those who wish to have a clearer and larger knowledge of the history of Russia and Russian mentality—a knowledge which is indispensable to the statesman who wishes, as we all do, to restore the bonds that formerly united Russia and Great Britain so closely."—*Morning Post*.

RUSSIA AND THE GREAT WAR

By Gregor Alexinsky. Demy 8vo, cloth, 10/6 net.

"M. Alexinsky is full of information and unexceptionable views generally of the most enlightened character."—*The Times.*

"M. Alexinsky has a good deal to tell us which, besides being solid and informing, is also encouraging and heartening."—*The Academy.*

THE SOUL OF EUROPE

A Character Study of the Militant Nations. By Joseph McCabe. Demy 8vo, cloth, 10/6 net.

"Mr. McCabe has written an illuminating and valuable book, which is all the more convincing since he is candid enough to admit the fine qualities which have been submerged in the havoc of this awful war."—*Standard.*

THE PSYCHOLOGY OF THE GREAT WAR

By Gustav Le Bon. Translated by E. Andrews, and with an Introduction specially written for the English edition by the author. Demy 8vo, cloth, 10/6 net.

"The book is an able and valuable survey of the war from many points of view, often very independent and original as we expect a book by M. Le Bon to be."—*Saturday Review.*

A SHORT HISTORY OF FRANCE

By Mary Duclaux (A. Mary F. Robinson). With 4 Maps. Demy 8vo, cloth, 10/6 net.

"It is written with a delightful ease and lightness of touch, and indicates very clearly the main lines of French national development from the beginning to the battle of Waterloo."—*Manchester Guardian.*

"Mme. Duclaux possesses the art of breathing life into the dry bones of the dead past."—*The Times.*

BEAUTIFUL BUILDINGS IN FRANCE AND BELGIUM

With 40 Monochrome and 10 coloured Illustrations, and Descriptive Notes by C. Harrison Townsend, F.R.I.B.A. Crown 4to, cloth, 10/6 net.

"No connoisseur but would delight in the possession of these reproductions in colour and monochrome from rare originals of the most beautiful buildings in France and Belgium, some now irreparably injured by German barbarity."—*Church Times.*

THE MONARCHY IN POLITICS

By J. A. Farrer, author of "Invasion and Conscription." Demy 8vo, cloth, 10/6 net.

"This book gives an account of the actual practical working of constitutional monarchy in Great Britain. An exceedingly useful as well as an exceedingly interesting book."—*Daily News.*

COURT AND DIPLOMACY IN AUSTRIA AND GERMANY: What I Know

By Countess Olga Leutrum. With 8 Illustrations. Demy 8vo, cloth, 10/6 net. [*Second Impression*

"Forms a not unworthy pendant to the famous Lichnowsky disclosures. We may even go further than this, and say that, as many of these admissions came from men of higher standing than the Ambassador to the Court of St. James's, they are of actually greater importance."—*Evening Standard.*

A WOMAN'S EXPERIENCES IN THE GREAT WAR

By Louise Mack (Mrs. Creed). Illustrated. Demy 8vo, cloth, 10/6 net.

"Mrs. Creed has written in this vivid book almost the best account which we have so far read of the desolation and havoc brought about in Belgium by the war."—*Standard.*

PROBLEMS OF RECONSTRUCTION

A Symposium by the Right Hon. W. H. Dickinson, M.P., Professor J. H. Muirhead, LL.D., Canon the Hon. E. Lyttleton, M.A., Sydney Webb, and others. With an Introduction by the Marquess of Crewe, K.G. Large Crown 8vo, cloth, 8/6 net.

The contents of this volume cover the whole field of reconstruction, national, international, social, religious, educational and artistic.

BRITAIN AFTER THE PEACE: Revolution or Reconstruction

By Brougham Villiers. Large Crown 8vo, cloth, 8/6 net.

Deals in a vigorous way with the problems of demobilisation, industrial control, taxation, agricultural reform and small holdings, the probable effects of the war in foreign countries, the foreign policy of the future, and the reaction of European politics on British problems.

CHANGING GERMANY

By Charles Tower. Large ·Crown 8vo, cloth, 7/6 net.

" It is one of the most intelligent attempts yet made to analyse the character and war behaviour of Germany."—*Evening Standard.*

THE PROBLEM OF HUMAN PEACE: Studied from the Standpoint of a Scientific Catholicism

By Malcolm Quin. Demy 8vo, cloth, 7/6 net.

"Mr. Quin attacks the question of how far it may be possible to prevent the recurrence of such a war as the present, and to maintain the lasting peace of the world."— *The Times.*

RELIGION IN EUROPE AND THE WORLD CRISIS

By Charles E. Osborne, author of " The Life of Father Dolling."   Demy 8vo, cloth, 7/6 net.

"The book is one of the most interesting, one of the most timely, and one of the most valuable we have read since war was declared. . . . Possesses qualities which will make it readable and valuable long after peace is declared."—*Manchester Guardian.*

THE PARTITIONS OF POLAND

By Lord Eversley.   With 4 Maps and 8 Illustrations. Demy 8vo, cloth, 7/6 net.   [*Second Impression*

"Thoroughness, dignity, and a calm, even judgment, are the conspicuous characteristics of Lord Eversley's study of the sufferings and wrongs of Poland during the last 150 years." —*Daily Telegraph.*

THE BOOK OF ITALY

Issued under the auspices of Her Majesty Queen Elena of Italy.   Edited by Raffaello Piccoli, D.Litt. With an Introduction by Viscount Bryce, O.M.   32 Half-tone and Line full-page Illustrations and 6 in Colour.   Cloth, 7/6 net.   Also a fine Edition, bound in white vellum with a gilt top, price 21/- net.

" Lovers of Italy will thrill to it, and it will win new lovers for Italy."—*The Times.*

AIRCRAFT AND THE GREAT WAR

By Claude Grahame-White and Harry Harper.   Demy 8vo, cloth, 7/6 net.

"The book is of more than ordinary interest to readers who wish to know how aerial warfare is being conducted, and how the aeroplane has triumphed in the first and most crucial test."—*Westminster Gazette.*

THE FUTURE OF THE DISABLED SOLDIER

By C. W. Hutt, M.A., M.D. Cantab., D.P.H. Oxon.
Recently Member of the War Pensions Committee.
Illustrated. Crown 8vo, cloth, 6/- net.

"Those who are anxious to help the disabled sailors and soldiers would do well to consult Dr. Hutt's book."—*Spectator*.

TURKEY AND THE WAR

By Vladimir Jabotinsky. Crown 8vo, cloth, 6/- net.

"M. Jabotinsky contends that the *causa causans* of this war is the problem of the Near and Middle East. . . . It is one of the very few war books that cannot be ignored by serious students of world politics."—*Manchester Guardian*.

INDUSTRIAL RECONSTRUCTION: A Symposium on the Situation after the War.

Edited by Huntley Carter. Crown 8vo, cloth, 6/- net.

"The whole subject is treated in a broad, reasonable spirit, and there is much that is far-seeing and helpfully suggestive in the tentative programmes that are laid down for re-building the world when peace returns to it."—*Bookman*.

A PRISONER OF THE GERMANS IN SOUTH-WEST AFRICA

By Percy L. Close. Crown 8vo, cloth, 6/- net.

The same disregard of international law, not to say ordinary humanity, characterised the treatment of prisoners in South-West Africa as has been the case in Germany itself. This is the plain unvarnished story of the experiences of 150 Britishers in captivity.

THE STORY OF THE NATIONS

For a clear understanding of the events which led up to the outbreak of hostilities a knowledge of the history of the nations concerned is necesssary. The first and best popular history of the world is the Story of the Nations series, and the volumes detailed below, dealing with the countries affected by the Great War, are recommended for present reading.

THE STORY OF THE NATIONS

Each volume is profusely illustrated and includes Maps
Large Crown 8vo, cloth, 5/- net each

MODERN ENGLAND (2 Vols.)
By Justin McCarthy.

MODERN FRANCE
By Andre Le Bon.

MODERN ITALY
By Prof. Pietro Orsi

MODERN SPAIN
By Martin A. S. Hume

IRELAND
By the Hon. Emily Lawless.

SCOTLAND
By John Macintosh, LL.D.

WALES
By Owen Edwards.

CANADA
By Sir John Bourniot, C.M.G

AUSTRALIAN COMMONWEALTH
By Greville Tregarthen

SOUTH AFRICA
By George McCall Theal.

BRITISH INDIA
By R W. Frazer.

PORTUGAL
By H. Morse Stephens, M.A

NORWAY
By Prof. Hjalmar H. Boyesen

DENMARK & SWEDEN
By Jon Stefansson.

GERMANY
By S. Baring Gould

HUNGARY
By Prof. Arminius Vambéry.

TURKEY
By Stanley Lane Poole.

BOHEMIA
By C. Edmund Maurice.

THE BALKANS
By W. Miller

AUSTRIA
By Sidney Whitman.

CHINA
By Prof. R. K. Douglas

JAPAN
By David Murray, Ph.D., LL.D.

POLAND
By W. R. Morfill, M.A.

RUSSIA
By W. R. Morfill, M.A.

SWITZERLAND
By Lina Hug & R. Stead.

PERSIA
By S G. W. Benjamin

HOLLAND
By Prof. J. E. Thorold Rogers

MEXICO
By Susan Hale

A complete list of " The Story of the Nations ' Series will be sent post free to any address on application to Mr. T. Fisher Unwin.

AMERICA AND GERMANY: A Textbook of the War

By J. William White, Ph.D., LL.D.   Large Crown 8vo, cloth, 5/- net.

"One of the most illuminating books the war has brought forth. . . . There is no reason for wonder that so lucid a statement of his case should attract and convince countless readers."—*Punch.*

FOR THE RIGHT: Essays and Addresses by Members of the Fight for Right Movement

Crown 8vo, cloth, 5/- net.

"Gives the reader the British national view of the problem of International relations. 'For the Right' is to be commended heartily to those who are in search of clear thinking on those abstract principles which, we claim, lie at the root of the Entente's action in this war."—*The New Europe.*

GERMAN CONSPIRACIES IN AMERICA. From an American Point of View

By William H. Skaggs.   With an Introduction by T. Andrea Cook.   Large Crown 8vo, cloth, 5/- net.

"Interesting the book is, from cover to cover, for Mr. Skaggs writes easily, forcefully, and with a complete knowledge of all the subjects he touches on."—*Sunday Times.*

THE GERMAN PERIL: Forecasts, 1864-1914. Realities, 1915. Hopes

By Frederick Harrison.   Large Cr. 8vo, cloth, 5/- net.

"There is perhaps, now living, no more intimate authority on the German question and the German menace than Mr. Harrison."—*Globe.*

THE KAISER: His Personality and Career

By Joseph McCabe, author of "The Soul of Europe," etc.   Crown 8vo, cloth, 5/- net.

"A short but able and forcible study.   Mr. McCabe believes that the Kaiser is not only responsible for the war, but directly responsible for the horrors of German military methods."—*The Times.*

THE MOTOR-BUS IN WAR

By A. M. Beatson.   Crown 8vo, cloth, 5/- net.

"Tells of the work of a mechanical transport column of the A.S.C. during more than three years of war. . . . It contains a multitude of good stories of the army's second line."—*Land and Water.*

SOUTH = WEST AFRICA (formerly German South-West Africa)

By William Eveleigh.   Crown 8vo, cloth, 5/- net.

"The book may be recommended as not only the best but the only English work dealing exclusively with this new addition to our oversea empire."—*Standard.*

A SHORT HISTORY OF BELGIUM AND HOLLAND

By Alexander Young.   Illustrated.   Cloth, 5/- net.

"Mr. Alexander Young has, in a great measure, done for our brave ally and the adjacent state what Green did for England."—*Globe.*

"Will be found to be a useful companion to Motley's brilliant history."—*Scottish Geographical Magazine.*

IN THE WHIRLPOOL OF WAR

By Isabelle Rimbaud.   Crown 8vo, cloth, 5/- net.

A particularly interesting description, in diary form, of the flight by road of a French lady and her invalid husband from Roche, in the Ardennes, to Paris at the time when the Germans were advancing to the Marne.

ITALY'S GREAT WAR AND HER NATIONAL ASPIRATIONS

With 20 Illustrations and 4 Maps.   Cloth, 5/- net.

This work is written by six prominent Italian publicists, and has an introductory chapter by H. Nelson Gay.   Among the subjects discussed are—Why Italy entered the War, National Aspirations, Strategic Problems in the Adriatic, and Economic and Financial Resources.

AN ALPHABET OF ECONOMICS

By A. R. Orage, editor of "The New Age." Crown 8vo, cloth, 4/6 net.

In view of the certainty that economic questions will occupy a prominent place during the coming reconstructive period in public discussions, a work such as this, at once popular and positive, is indispensable to the student of affairs.

A FRENCHMAN'S THOUGHTS ON THE WAR

By Paul Sabatier, author of "The Life of St. Francis of Assisi." Crown 8vo, cloth, 4/6 net.

M. Paul Sabatier regards the present war as the revolt of the human conscience against the bleak materialism and over-whelming self-assertion of Germany.

HUMANITY *VERSUS* UNHUMANITY: A Criticism of the German Idea in its Political and Philosophical Development

By A. S. Elwell-Sutton. Crown 8vo, cloth, 4/6 net.

"The author's study of German thought and German development is well done. His book is one to be read with profit." —*Daily Telegraph.*

POTENTIAL RUSSIA

By Richard Washburn Child. Crown 8vo, cloth, 4/6 net.

"Mr. Child has studied closely the lives and ideas of the people."—*Observer.*

"Interesting because it records the impressions of an unusually acute observer."—*Manchester Guardian.*

WAR AND THE IDEAL OF PEACE

By Henry Rutgers Marshall. Crown 8vo, cloth, 4/6 net.

A study of those characteristics of man that result in war, and of the means by which they may be controlled.

DEMOCRACY AT THE CROSS ROADS

By Maude Petre. Crown 8vo, cloth, 4/6 net.

Though a convinced democrat, the author has here written what may in part be regarded as a homily addressed to labour.

Contents :—I. The Safety of Democracy the Safety of the World. II. Leadership. III. Citizenship. IV. Dreamers, Thinkers and Idealists. V. The Religion of Democracy. VI. Woman's Part in the New World.

ARMS AND THE MAP: A Study of Nationalities and Frontiers

By Ian C. Hannah, M.A. Crown 8vo, cloth, 3/6 net.

"A readable presentation of the problems of irredentist lands and peoples. The author has worked skilfully into his book knowledge of peculiarly timely interest." — *Geographical Review*.

THE BRITISH SOLDIER: His Courage and Humour

By E. J. Hardy. Crown 8vo, cloth, 3/6 net.

" Gives an intimate insight into the ways and manners, the humour and devotion of those actually engaged in the fighting line."—*Globe*.

FRIENDLY RUSSIA

By Denis Garstin. With an Introduction by H. G. Wells. Crown 8vo, cloth, 3/6 net.

"Mr. Garstin gives an interesting description of the home life and customs of the Russian people which should do much to enlighten readers as to the real position of Russia."—*Outlook*.

THE GERMAN CHANCELLOR AND THE OUTBREAK OF WAR

By J. W. Headlam, author of " The History of Twelve Days." Demy 8vo, cloth, 3/6 net.

"This is, in effect, a supplement to the valuable analysis of the diplomatic negotiations immediately preceding the entry of Great Britain into the War, which Mr. Headlam issued under the title 'The History of Twelve Days.'"—*The Times*.

A HISTORY OF THE ROYAL WELSH
FUSILIERS (late 23rd Regiment)

By Howel Thomas. With 4 Illustrations. Cloth, 3/6 net.

The Regiment's glorious record is told by a writer who knows how to arrange his story and to hold the reader's interest.

INSTINCTS OF THE HERD IN PEACE AND WAR

By W. Trotter. Crown 8vo, cloth, 3/6 net.

" It is a balanced and an inspiring study of one of the prime factors of human advance."—*The Times.*

LLOYD GEORGE : The Man and his Story

By Frank Dilnot. With 2 Portraits. Crown 8vo, cloth, 3/6 net.

" Mr. Dilnot has given us a fascinating volume full of human interest throughout, inspiring and stimulating." — *Welsh Outlook.*

" A fascinating sketch of the personality of the Premier."— *Daily Graphic.*

THE HELL-GATE OF SOISSONS AND OTHER POEMS ("The Song of the Guns")

By Herbert Kaufman. Crown 8vo, cloth, 3/6 net.

"Shows a wonderful penetration into popular feeling in England and the Colonies in regard to the magnificent achievements of our 'Tommies' at the front, their heroism and their humour."—*Book Monthly.*

RHYMES OF A RED-CROSS MAN

By Robert W. Service, author of " Songs of a Sourdough," etc. Crown 8vo, cloth, 3/6 net.

" It is the great merit of Mr. Service's verses that they are literally alive with the stress and joy, and agony and hardship, that make up life out in the battle zone. He has never written better than in this book, and that is saying a great deal."—*Bookman.*

WHY DON'T THEY CHEER? AND OTHER CANADIAN POEMS

By Robert J. C. Stead.   Crown 8vo, cloth, 3/6 net.

"Contains some of the best ballads and lyrics that have been written in honour of Canada's fighting men. . . . . Altogether a very notable book of verse."—*The Bookman.*

SVEN HEDIN—NOBLEMAN

By K. G. Ossiannilsson.   Crown 8vo, cloth, 3/6 net.

"An effective exposure of Mr. Sven Hedin as a pro-German of a virulent type."—*Spectator.*

MONTENEGRO : In History, Politics and War

By Alex. Devine.   With a Map.   Crown 8vo, cloth, 3/6 net.

Mr. Devine has had exceptional opportunities for studying his subject, and the result is a work both informing and fascinating.

RASPUTIN : Prophet, Libertine, Plotter

By T. Vogel-Jörgensen.   Crown 8vo, cloth, 3/6 net.

"The career of the hypocritical scoundrel who did so much to ruin Russia is related by a neutral writer in half-a-dozen deeply interesting chapters."—*Literary Guide.*

PRO PATRIA.   A Guide to Public and Personal Service in War Time.

Edited by T. M. Kelynack, M.D.   Cloth, 3/6 net.

SOME ASPECTS OF THE WAR

By S. Perez Triana, formerly of the Permanent Court of Arbitration at the Hague.   Crown 8vo, cloth, 3/6 net.

"It will prove a very valuable textbook to the student of the events that led to the great European conflagration."—·*Globe.*

QUESTIONS OF WAR AND PEACE

By L. T. Hobhouse, D.Litt., author of "The World in Conflict." Crown 8vo, cloth, 3/6 net.

"In these brilliant platonic dialogues on current questions Professor Hobhouse has provided us with a delightful entertainment."—*Spectator*.

"An important contribution to the philosophy of the war."—*Daily Telegraph*.

HOW FRANCE IS GOVERNED

By M. Raymond Poincaré. Popular edition. Large Crown 8vo, cloth, 3/6 net.

"It gives an insight into the government of France such as one can gain nowhere else."—*Quarterly Review*.

"The book will take its place among the standard authorities on constitutional government."—*Journal of Education*.

THE GOVERNANCE OF ENGLAND

By Sidney Low, B.A. Revised and with a new Introduction. Large Crown 8vo, cloth, 3/6 net.

"Mr. Low's work has won the recognition of a standard authority, and the deserved rank of an educational textbook in this and in other countries."—*Pall Mall Gazette*.

"Occupies a special place in the regard of the political student."—*Standard*.

FRIGHTFULNESS IN THEORY AND PRACTICE, AS COMPARED WITH FRANCO-BRITISH WAR USAGES

Translated from the French of Charles Andler, with additions by the Editor, Bernard Miall. Crown 8vo, cloth, 2/6 net.

"Nowhere will you get a clearer picture of the laws and conventions which pretend to mitigate the horrors of German warfare, and the insolent manner in which even these paltry limitations are disregarded."—*New Witness*.

IN A FRENCH HOSPITAL : Notes of a Nurse

By M. Eydoux-Demians. Crown 8vo, cloth, 2/6 net.

"A fine impression of the spirit of the French nation in this war is to be gained from this book."—*The Times.*

"It is a beautiful little book."—*Tatler.*

LORD KITCHENER : His Work and his Prestige

By Henry D. Davray. With an Introduction by Paul Cambon, French Ambassador. Crown 8vo, cloth, 2/6 net. [*Second Impression*

"The well-known French *littérateur* gives us a graphic and effective portrayal of Kitchener's work. M. Davray followed events in England closely and on the spot."—*The Times.*

MILITARISM AT WORK IN BELGIUM AND GERMANY

By K. G. Ossiannilsson. Crown 8vo, cloth, 2/6 net.

"A damning exposure, carefully based on documentary evidence, of the German policy of deporting Belgian workmen and the working of the Preventive Arrest Law in Germany."—*Land and Water.*

THE SECRET PRESS IN BELGIUM

By Jean Massart, author of "Belgians under the German Eagle." Illustrated. Crown 8vo, 2/6 net.

"A spirited account of the way in which the Belgians have used the printing press to support their passive resistance to the brutal and stupid German rule."—*Spectator.*

WHO IS RIGHT IN THE WORLD WAR

By K. G. Ossiannilsson. Crown 8vo, cloth, 2/6 net.

"The author gives a refreshingly frank opinion to his fellow countrymen, the Swedes, on the subject of the war."—*Contemporary Review.*

THE PSYCHOLOGY OF THE KAISER

By Morton Prince, LL.D., author of "The American *versus* The German View of the War." Crown 8vo, cloth, 2/6 net.

Deals with the Kaiser's divine right illusion, his monomania in regard to German autocracy and the army, and his violent antipathy to the Social-Democratic party.

WITH THE RUSSIAN WOUNDED

By Tatiana Alexinsky. Translated by Gilbert Cannan. With a Preface by G. Alexinsky. Crown 8vo, cloth, 2/6 net.

"Short, vivid diary records; full of the personal note, and flashing the individual tragedies of war before the eyes."—*The Times.*

EUROPEAN INTERNATIONAL RELATIONS

By J. A. Murray Macdonald, M.P. Crown 8vo, cloth, 2/6 net.

"It is one of the few constructive books which so far have appeared that will survive the war."—*Contemporary Review.*

THE NEW PROTECTIONISM

By J. A Hobson, author of "Work and Wealth," etc. Crown 8vo, cloth, 2/6 net.

A critical examination of the economic proposals discussed at the Paris Conference, written with the author's masterly ability.

"It is a ruthless and unsparing piece of criticism."—*Daily News.*

THE LAST LINE AND OTHER POEMS

By E. Vine Hall. Crown 8vo, cloth, 2/6 net.

"Mr. Vine Hall has written war verses that are both effective and sincere."—*Aberdeen Press.*

"Full of charm."—*Oxford Magazine.*

DICTIONARY OF NAVAL AND MILITARY TERMS. With Names and Description of the Principal Ships in the British Navy, etc.

By C. F. Tweney, F.F.A.   Cloth, 2/6 net.

"The kind of book that should be in the hands of everyone interested in the war—and who is not?"—*Librarian.*

THE FUTURE OF MILITARISM

An Examination of Oliver's "Ordeal by Battle."   By "Roland" (the Right Hon. J. M. Robertson, M.P). Crown 8vo, cloth, 2/6 net.   [*Second Impression*

"It is a masterly piece of reasoning and a piece of clever writing—by far the best controversial book on the war."—*Daily Chronicle.*

HOSPITAL DAYS

By "Platoon Commander," author of "With My Regiment."   Crown 8vo, cloth, 2/6 net.

"A well-written, cheery, humorous account by an officer of his experiences of being wounded and of life in hospital in England."—*New Statesman.*

GERMAN ATROCITIES. An Official Investigation

By J. H. Morgan, M.A., late Home Office Commissioner with the British Expeditionary Force.   Demy 8vo, cloth, 2/- net (paper edition, 1/- net).

"No more appalling indictment against a nation and its governors could well be framed than is to be found in 'German Atrocities.'"—*Daily Telegraph.*

THE RUSSIAN REVOLUTION AND WHO'S WHO IN RUSSIA

By Zinovy N. Preev, editor of "Twentieth Century Russia."   Crown 8vo, cloth, 2/- net.

TREITSCHKE AND THE GREAT WAR

By Joseph McCabe.   Crown 8vo, cloth, 2/- net.

"Mr. McCabe gives us a very lucid picture of the great teacher of Germany, and the points of resemblance and difference between him and Nietzsche."—*Evening Standard.*

FROM THE TRENCHES. Louvain to the Aisne

By Geoffrey Young.   Crown 8vo, paper covers, 2/- net.

"The first account of an eye-witness of the first phases of the Great War in the western area.   The work is vivid and realistic."—*Land and Water.*

THE A B C OF MILITARY LAW.   A Concise Guide for the Use of Officers, N.C.O. and Men

By Capt. Francis D. Grierson.   Demy 16mo, cloth, 1/6 net.

"An invaluable little manual."—*Daily Graphic.*

GERMANY AND SPAIN : The Views of a Spanish Catholic

By Conde F. Melgar.   Crown 8vo, cloth, 1/6 net.

"The fifteen sections of the pamphlet form a severe indictment, and present to the world some damning facts which should have their influence on all supporters of reason and students of history."—*Saturday Review.*

A SHORT COURSE OF PHYSICAL TRAINING

By Allan Broman, Principal of the London Central Institute for Swedish Gymnastics.   Fully Illustrated. Cloth, limp, 1/6 net.

WHAT THE IRISH REGIMENTS HAVE DONE

By S. Parnell Kerr.   With a Diary of a Visit to the Front by John E. Redmond.   Crown 8vo, cloth, 1/6 net ; paper cover, 1/- net.

"Here are stories that thrill, stories of bravery and pathos that Ireland can never forget."—*Evening Standard.*

BROTHER TOMMY

By M. M. Henry Ruffin and Andre Tudesq. Paper cover, 1/3 net.

A French account of the British Army's doings in France during the first half of last year.

THE BRITISH ARMY AT WAR

By Frank Fox, R.F.A., author of "The Agony of Belgium." Illustrated. Paper cover, 1/- net.

This book gives a general impression of the extent and variety of the work of the British Army.

THE AMERICAN *VERSUS* THE GERMAN VIEW OF THE WAR

By Morton Prince. Crown 8vo, paper cover, 1/- net.

"It would be impossible to find a more convincing and crushing, nay, annihilating, exposure of the German case than Dr. Morton Prince's pamphlet."—*Spectator.*

AMERICA'S ARRAIGNMENT OF GERMANY

By J. William White, Ph.D., LL.D. Crown 8vo, cloth, 1/- net.

"Considering its size this is one of the most businesslike and cogent 'arraignments' of Germany that we have seen."— *The Times.*

CLEARED FOR ACTION (Songs of the Navy).

By Harwood Steele. Cloth, 1/- net.

"A book in a navy blue cover that is, at this moment, better than meat or drink or anything printed—except good news." —*Westminster Gazette.*

THE ENTENTE CORDIALE IN LEBANON

By Prince Tyan. With a Frontispiece. Paper cover, 1/- net.

'This pamphlet is an eloquent—and thoroughly Oriental—plea for consideration of the position of the Lebanon by France and England."—*The Near East.*

DOCUMENTS OF THE GREAT WAR

Collected by Giuseppe A. Andruilli. Translated and with an Introduction by Thomas Okey, and with a Preface by Guglielmo Ferrero. Crown 8vo, cloth, 1/- net.

" The documents, impartially collected and accurately translated, carry their own damning indictment of a wanton agression by Germany."—*Nation*.

FIVE HUNDRED AND ONE GEMS OF GERMAN THOUGHT

Selected by William Archer. Paper cover, 1/- net.

A collection of extracts from a great number of sources illustrating German tendencies to national self-glorification.

THE GERMAN PERIL AND THE GRAND ALLIANCE : How to Crush Prussian Militarism

By G. de Wesselitsky. Paper cover, 1/- net.

This is the text of a lecture to the Russia Society, presided over by the Speaker of the House of Commons. M. de Wesselitsky has made a lifelong study of Germany and her history.

THE KAISER UNDER THE SEARCHLIGHT

By A. H. Catling. Paper cover, 1/- net.

" Gives vivid pictures of the German Emperor in his various aspects. . . . A valuable contribution to our knowledge of the Kaiser."—*Academy*.

THE GERMANS IN CORK

Being the letters of His Excellency the Baron von Kartoffel and others. Paper cover, 1/- net.

A collection of letters supposed to be written during a German occupation of Ireland. It is a clever and amusing piece of satire.

LIFE IN A GERMAN CRACK REGIMENT

By Baron von Schlicht (Baron von Baudissin). Paper cover, 1/- net.

This book is a startling indictment of German military manners and morals.

THE MEANING OF THE WAR: Life and Matter in Conflict

By Henri Bergson. With an Introduction by H. Wildon Carr. Crown 8vo, cloth, 1/- net.

"In its precision of statement and its clear insight into the radical difference between the cause of Germany and that of the Allies, it is one of the most suggestive contributions to thought which the world has produced."—*Inquirer*.

THE ROLLER BANDAGE

By Howard M. Preston, Demonstrator of the Practical Ambulance Classes at the Polytechnic, Regent Street. With an Introduction by James Cantlie, M.A., M.B., F.R.C.S., and 160 figures. Paper cover, 1/- net.

THE TRIANGULAR BANDAGE

The Application of the Triangular Bandage shown by Words and Diagrams. By Howard M. Preston. With an Introduction by James Cantlie, M.A., M.B., F.R.C.S. Fully Illustrated, with 116 figures. Paper cover, 1/- net.

QUICK RIFLE TRAINING FOR NATIONAL DEFENCE

By E. H. Stone. Illustrated with Diagrams. Cloth, 1/- net.

"A lucid and readable account of the main features of military rifle training."— *Spectator*.

SOLDIER SONGS FROM ANZAC

By Signaller Tom Skeyhill. With an Introduction by Major-General J. W. McCoy, C.B. Paper cover, 1/- net.

"A collection of rugged dialect ballads, in which all the Australian fighting man's qualities, especially his grim, unconquerable humour, shine with the brightness of naked steel."—*Morning Post*.

SIXTY AMERICAN OPINIONS ON THE WAR

By Representative Citizens. Crown 8vo, cloth, 1/- net.

"The cream of the intellectual life of the Republic speaks in these vibrating pages, and from end to end of the volume the voice is on the side of freedom and against Germany."—*Pall Mall Gazette*.

THE TRUTH ABOUT THE WAR

By Alvaro Alcala Galiano. Paper cover, 1/- net.

"This translation of the appeal of a Spanish writer to his countrymen will enable Englishmen to gain a clear idea of the opposing influences which mould Spanish opinion on the war."—*The Times*.

THE WORLD IN CONFLICT

By L. T. Hobhouse, author of "Questions of War and Peace." Crown 8vo, cloth, 1/- net.

A study of the psychological causes of the war.

"It will have a documentary value for the future historical student as well as an educational value in the present."—*Manchester Guardian*.

WAR SPEECHES BY BRITISH MINISTERS, 1914-1916

Paper cover, 1/- net.

This volume gives a picture of the activities of the two administrations over which Mr. Asquith presided.

WAR'S ECHO. Poems

By Ronald Gurner. Paper cover, 1/- net.

"The author has succeeded in recording some of the impressions formed amid the tempest of war."—*Athenæum*.

NEUTRALITY *VERSUS* JUSTICE. An Essay on International Relations

By A. J. Jacobs. Paper cover, 1/- net.

"Mr. Jacobs has many things to say which are worth reading."—*Arbitrator*.

A SHORT ACCOUNT OF THE GERMAN INVASION AND OCCUPATION OF BELGIUM

By Leon van der Essen. Small Crown 8vo, paper cover, 1/- net.

IRELAND, FRANCE, AND PRUSSIA

A Selection from the Speeches and Writings of John Mitchel. With an Introduction by J. de L. Smyth. Paper cover, 8d. net.

ALSACE UNDER GERMAN RULE

By Maître Paul Albert Helmer. Paper cover, 6d. net.

In this pamphlet, by a distinguished Alsatian lawyer, the German treatment of the country since 1871 is discussed, together with its reaction on the inhabitants.

WOMAN AND WAR

By Olive Schreiner, from "Woman and Labour." Paper cover, 6d. net.

In "Woman and War" Miss Schreiner gives her views on one of the most vital questions of the day.

THE TRUE AND THE FALSE PACIFICISM

By Count Goblet d'Alviella, Vice-President of the Belgian Senate. Paper cover, 6d. net.

THE REAL GERMAN RIVALRY: Yesterday, To-day, and To-Morrow

By Sir Swire Smith, M.P., LL.D. Second and cheaper edition. Paper cover, 6d. net.

"Sir Swire Smith has always been a keen champion of technical education, and it is in training and education that he finds the real arena wherein we have to fight the Germans." —*The Times*.

WHAT THE BRITISH EMPIRE IS DOING IN THE WAR

By Briggs Davenport. Paper cover, 6d. net.

SIGNOR SALANDRA'S GREAT SPEECH, June 2, 1915. A Vindication of Italian Policy

Translated, and with an Introductory Note, by Thomas Okey. Paper cover, 6d. net.

States in clear language Italy's reasons for unsheathing the sword and ranging herself upon the side of the Allies.

BRITAIN *VERSUS* GERMANY

An Open Letter to Professor Edward Meyer, of the University of Berlin. By the Right Hon. J. M. Robertson, M.P. Paper cover, 6d. net.

THE BRITISH EMPIRE AND THE WAR

By E. A. Benians. Paper cover, 6d. net.

Mr. Benians writes with insight and knowledge of the development, significance and future of the British Empire as studied from the point of view of the present war.

THE GROUNDWORK OF CONSCRIPTION

An Epitome of the Military Service Code in Great Britain, with the disciplinary measures, civil and military, for its enforcement. By G. Gavan Duffy, B.L. Paper cover, 6d. net.

PAMPHLETS

An important series of Pamphlets dealing with various
phases and incidents of the Great War

IN PAPER COVERS, PRICES NET

BRITAIN TRANSFORMED. New Industries Illustrated. 6d.

TO THE ITALIAN ARMIES. By Jules Destrée and Richard
Dupierreux. 6d.

BRITISH WORKSHOPS AND THE WAR. By the Right Hon.
Christopher Addison, M.P. 3d.

REPORTS ON BRITISH PRISON CAMPS IN INDIA AND
BURMA. Visited by the International Red Cross Committee in
February, March and April, 1917. 3d.

THE GATHERING OF THE CLANS. By J. Saxon Mills. New
and Enlarged Edition. Illustrated. 3d.

ENGLAND AND HER CRITICS. By Mario Borsa. 3d.

GERMAN RULE IN AMERICA. By Evans Lewin. 3d.

NEUTRALS AND THE WAR. By the Right Hon. J. M.
Robertson, M.P. 2d.

THE VILLAIN OF THE WORLD TRAGEDY. By William
Archer 2d.

SIX OF ONE AND HALF-A-DOZEN OF THE OTHER. A
Letter to Mr. L. Simons, of the Hague. By William Archer. 2d.

MORAL ASPECTS OF THE EUROPEAN WAR. By Henrique
Lopes de Mendonça. 2d.

GREAT BRITAIN'S SEA POLICY. By Prof. Gilbert Murray. 2d.

GERMAN BUSINESS AND GERMAN AGGRESSION. 2d.

CANADA TO IRELAND. By A. M. Drysdale. 2d.

GENERAL VON BISSING'S TESTAMENT: A Study in German Ideals. 2d.

MURDER AT SEA. By Archibald Hurd. 2d.

THE FINANCES OF GREAT BRITAIN AND GERMANY. By
E. F. Davies. 2d.

SOME AMERICAN OPINIONS ON THE INDIAN EMPIRE.
By Theodore Roosevelt, William Howard Taft, E. Jeffreys,
Admiral Goodrich, James M Hubbard, and others. 2d.

THE STRAIGHT PATH AND THE CROOKED. 2d.

THE ACHIEVEMENTS OF THE ZEPPELINS. By A. Swede. 2d.

THE MORAL BASIS OF ITALY'S WAR. By GIORGIO DEL VECCHIO. 2d.

THE DEPORTATIONS OF BELGIAN WORKMEN. By JULES DESTRÉE. 2d.

BRITAIN'S CASE AGAINST GERMANY. By the late Rev. H. M. GWATKIN. Reprinted from the *Nation*. 1d.

GERMAN TRUTH AND A MATTER OF FACT. By the Right Hon. J. M. ROBERTSON, M.P. 1d.

BLOOD AND BRASS. A Booklet of Quotations from German Statesmen, Soldiers, Philosophers and Clergymen. By WILLIAM ARCHER. 1d.

THE MEN WHO TIDY UP. By One who has served in a British Labour Battalion. 1d.

THE HORRORS OF ALEPPO. 1d.

THE "SINCERE CHANCELLOR." By FERNAND PASSELECQ. 1d.

THE WORKERS' RESOLVE. An interview with W. A. APPLETON, Secretary of the General Federation of Trade Unions. 1d.

THE CONDITION OF THE BELGIAN WORKMEN NOW REFUGEES IN ENGLAND. 1d.

THE OTTOMAN DOMINATION. 1d.

THE CHALLENGE ACCEPTED : President Wilson's Address to Congress, April 2nd, 1917. 1d.

A FREE FUTURE FOR THE WORLD. A Speech by the Right Hon. H. H. ASQUITH, M.P., at the Guildhall on Nov. 9, 1916. 1d.

THE WAR ON GERMAN SUBMARINES : Sir Edward Carson on the British Navy's Success. 1d.

THE GERMAN NOTE & THE REPLY OF THE ALLIES. 1d.

THE WORLD'S LARGEST LOAN. 1d.

THE DEPORTATIONS. Statement by the American Minister to Belgium. 1d.

THE WAR ON HOSPITAL SHIPS. 1d.

TO THE MEN BEHIND THE ARMIES. By EMILE CAMMAERTS. 1d.

A JAPANESE VIEW OF THE WAR. By Rear-Admiral AKIYAMA. 1d.

IRELAND & POLAND : A Comparison. By T. W. ROLLESTON. 1d.

THE MEANS OF VICTORY. A Speech by the Right Hon. EDWIN MONTAGU, M.P. 1d.

WHY BRITAIN IS IN THE WAR, and What She Hopes from the Future. A Speech by the Right Hon. VISCOUNT GREY. 1d.

SLAVE RAIDS IN BELGIUM. Facts about the Deportations. By J. VAN DER HEUVEL. 2d.

MAPS OF WAR AREAS

The most reliable Maps and Plans of the territory affected by the Great War, including the frontiers of neutral countries adjoining, will be found in Baedeker's Guides. These Maps and Plans are just as valuable for military purposes now, as they were to the tourist and traveller in the days of peace.

BAEDEKER GUIDE BOOKS

SPECIALLY RECOMMENDED FOR ARMY USE

AUSTRIA-HUNGARY, including DALMATIA and BOSNIA. With excursions to CETINJE, BELGRADE and BUCHAREST. With 71 Maps and 77 Plans and 2 Panoramas. Eleventh edition, revised and augmented. 1911. 10s. net.

THE EASTERN ALPS, including the BAVARIAN HIGHLANDS, TYROL, SALZBURG, UPPER and LOWER AUSTRIA, STYRIA, CARINTHIA, and CARNIOLA. With 73 Maps, 16 Plans, and 11 Panoramas. Twelfth edition, revised and augmented. 1911. 10s. net.

BELGIUM and HOLLAND, including the GRAND-DUCHY OF LUXEMBOURG. With 19 Maps and 45 Plans. Fifteenth edition, revised and augmented. 1910. 6s. net.

PARIS and its Environs, with Routes from LONDON to PARIS. With 14 Maps and 42 Plans. Eighteenth revised edition. 1913. 6s. net.

BERLIN and its Environs. With 7 Maps and 24 Plans. Fifth edition. 1912. 3s. net.

NORTHERN GERMANY, as far as the BAVARIAN and AUSTRIAN FRONTIERS. With 54 Maps and 101 Plans. Sixteenth revised edition. 1913. 8s. net.

SOUTHERN GERMANY (WURTEMBERG and BAVARIA). With 36 Maps and 45 Plans. Eleventh revised edition. 1910. 6s. net.

THE RHINE from ROTTERDAM to CONSTANCE, including the SEVEN MOUNTAINS, the MOSELLE, the VOLCANIC EIFEL, the TAUNUS, the ODENWALD AND HEIDELBERG, the VOSGES MOUNTAINS, the BLACK FOREST, &c. With 69 Maps and 59 Plans. Seventeenth revised edition. 1911. 8s. net.

GREECE, the GREEK ISLANDS, and an excursion to CRETE. With 16 Maps, 30 Plans, and a Panorama of ATHENS. Fourth revised edition. 1909. 8s. net.

NORWAY, SWEDEN & DENMARK, with excursions to ICELAND and SPITZBERGEN. With 62 Maps, 42 Plans, and 3 Panoramas. Tenth edition. 1912. 8s. net.

SWITZERLAND, and the adjacent portions of ITALY, SAVOY and TYROL. With 77 Maps, 21 Plans, and 15 Panoramas. Twenty-fifth edition. 1913. 8s. net.

NORTHERN ITALY, including LEGHORN, FLORENCE, RAVENNA, and routes through SWITZERLAND and AUSTRIA. With 36 Maps and 45 Plans. Fourteenth remodelled edition. 1913. 8s. net.

MSS.
MR. T. FISHER UNWIN is always glad to consider manuscripts — whether original works of fiction, poetry, philosophy, and other branches of literature, or documents of historical, biographical or literary interest—with a view to publication, and gives careful and prompt attention to all material submitted for that purpose.

Address all Letters and MSS. to

T. FISHER UNWIN, Ltd., 1 Adelphi Terrace, London, Eng.

MA.B.
(MAINLY ABOUT BOOKS)

Published Monthly, 1d.

M.A.B. is an illustrated magazine for book-buyers and book-readers. Each issue contains an interesting "London Letter" giving biographical notes with photographs of authors. It gives also excerpts from the most important books of the month, and specimen illustrations.

Specimen copy free. Annual subscription, 1s. post free

T. FISHER UNWIN, Ltd., 1 Adelphi Terrace, London, Eng.

Mr. T. FISHER UNWIN invites readers of this Catalogue to send for a copy of his latest announcement list of new books. Sent post free on application.

T. FISHER UNWIN, Ltd., 1 Adelphi Terrace, London, Eng.

Lightning Source UK Ltd.
Milton Keynes UK
UKHW02n0335020618
323616UK00005B/66/P